A poster for the New York & Boston Railroad reminds the public that only one route gives them a view of the great Niagara Falls on their trip west.

COVER: *The age of steel gave new power to the railroads, helping them to expand into full day and night service to meet the country's growing needs.*

FRONT ENDSHEET: *On the occasion of the World's Fair in Philadelphia in 1876, a "centennial mirror" reflected 100 years of progress in the United States.*

CONTENTS PAGE: *The Brotherhood of Locomotive Engineers, founded in April, 1863, as the first railroad union, gave this certificate to each member.*

BACK ENDSHEET: *An 1895 painting of the Bethlehem, Pennsylvania, steel plant shows a Bessemer converter (background) and workers pouring molten steel.*

*"A knowledge of the past prepares us for the crisis
of the present and the challenge of the future."*

JOHN F. KENNEDY
From his special foreword in Volume 1

THE AMERICAN HERITAGE
NEW ILLUSTRATED HISTORY
OF THE UNITED STATES

VOLUME 10

AGE OF STEEL

By ROBERT G. ATHEARN
Professor of History, University of Colorado

CREATED AND DESIGNED BY THE EDITORS OF
AMERICAN HERITAGE
The Magazine of History

PUBLISHED BY
DELL PUBLISHING CO., INC., NEW YORK

CONTENTS OF THE COMPLETE SERIES

Foreword by JOHN F. KENNEDY
Introduction by ALLAN NEVINS
Main text by ROBERT G. ATHEARN

A MASTER INDEX FOR ALL 16 VOLUMES APPEARS IN VOLUME 16

CONTENTS OF VOLUME 10

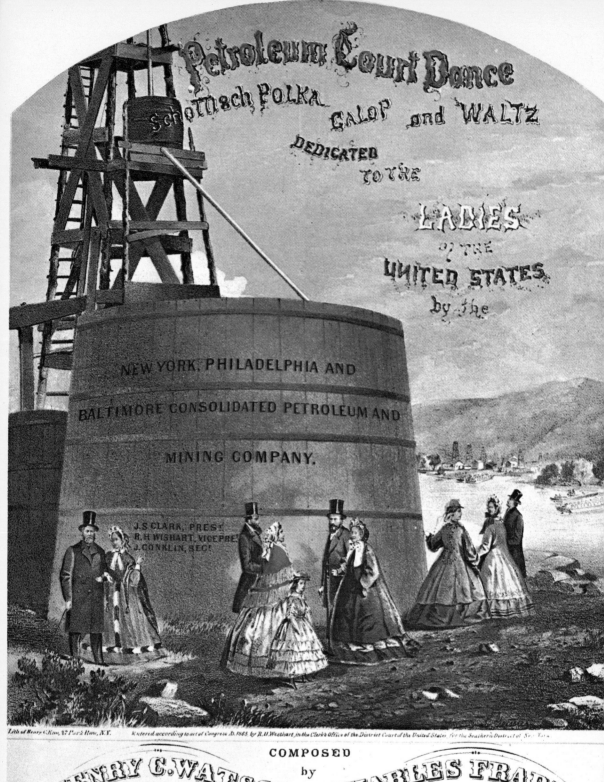

CHAPTER 28

INDUSTRIAL AMERICA

The guns of the Civil War were stilled, the banners were furled, and the survivors made their way homeward. The Confederate veteran found a ruined land. To Carl Schurz, a former Union general touring the South for President Andrew Johnson, the countryside "looked for many miles like a broad black streak of ruin and desolation." By contrast, the North had shot ahead. "Everywhere wartime industrialization had brought signs of growth," John Hope Franklin wrote. "What Union soldier could not quicken his pace as he moved not only nearer his loved ones but also closer to what would surely be a glorious future!"

For if the war had left many a sleeve empty and many a home bereaved, it had also left the nation a precious legacy—the North's magnificent industrial machine. The time for running it at full speed had never been better. From its beginnings a decade before, the Republican Party had adopted the businessman. For half a

In 1865, six years after the first well was drilled, an oil firm dedicated these dances to the ladies of the United States.

century after the war, it would continue to nurture him with favorable tariff, banking, railroad, and immigration legislation, and with all manner of general favors. Underlying this auspicious political climate was nature's bounteous inheritance. Copper, iron, oil, coal, gold, silver, timber, and almost limitless free land awaited exploitation. Virtually untouched before mid-century, the American West was a rich empire filled with treasures. Add to all this the human component —a bold group of entrepreneurs to mine the treasures, inventors and scientists to provide them with tools— and there emerged a combination bound to produce an economic revolution.

Andrew Carnegie, John D. Rockefeller, James J. Hill, William K. Vanderbilt—yes, even Jim Fisk and John W. "Bet You a Million" Gates —merely to repeat the names is to call up one of the gaudiest eras in American history.

The rich empire that awaited exploitation was not easy to subdue. It was a vast land of high mountains, rushing rivers, and climates that could be devastatingly cruel. Often the treasures were buried deep in the ground or located in places well-nigh inaccessible from established centers of population and production. A wrong guess—or a forest fire or a severe snowstorm—could make the difference between wealth and ruin. And in the absence of the type of regulatory legislation that we know today, the development of these resources was a dog-eat-dog business. "Indeed, under present-day rules," Stewart H. Holbrook has written, "[many of these industrialists] would face a good hundred years in prison.... These were tough-minded fellows, who fought their way encased in rhinoceros hides and filled the air with their mad bellowings and the cries of the wounded. . . ." Yet together they built an era that as much as any other has made America great.

The steel industry and its master, Andrew Carnegie, thoroughly exemplify the age and its spirit. The Kelley-Bessemer process, a cheap method of reducing molten pig iron into refined steel, was perfected during the 1850s, when Carnegie, a poor Scottish immigrant's son, was finding his feet in the New World as a bobbin boy and messenger in Pennsylvania. Simultaneously, huge deposits of iron ore were discovered in the great Mesabi Range of northern Minnesota.

Carnegie entered the steel industry shortly after the Civil War, and within 15 years reached the top. In 1882, he pooled his interests with Henry Clay Frick, who dominated the coke industry in Pittsburgh, and together they gained control of all the Mesabi Range ore they needed. From that point on, their only problem was competition, which they handled with ruthless aplomb.

A story with different characters but the same plot can be told of the oil industry. When "Colonel" E. L. Drake struck oil at Titusville, Pennsylvania, in 1859, the rush for "black gold" was on. Hundreds of prospectors sank wells, but a shrewd young commission merchant named John Davison Rockefeller was to make the most money. In 1860, he invested his savings of $700; in two years his stake became $4,000. In 1870, Rockefeller and some associates formed the Standard Oil Company of Ohio, capitalized at $1,000,000.

Standard Oil is a prime example of industrial success in the growing nation. After 1870, clear of debt and obligated to no one, it began to buy up smaller producers or force them to the wall. Growth meant power. The company now connected its expanding units with pipelines, thus not only increasing efficiency but forcing the railroads to submit to Standard Oil's demands. Soon the railroads were conspiring with Standard, to the ruin of other petroleum producers. Because it got secret rebates, or "kickbacks," on tank-car shipments, Rockefeller's company could deal fatal blows to its competitors.

By 1881, the policy of independence and maintenance of cash reserves pro-

In an 1866 photograph, Edwin L. Drake (wearing a top hat) stands near the world's first oil well, which he drilled in 1859 at Titusville, Pennsylvania.

duced a working backlog of $45,000,-000. The Standard Oil Trust was established and began to draw banks and railroads into its web. By 1895, its cash assets amounted to $150,000,000.

Alongside the names of Carnegie and Rockefeller stood those of other big-business captains. Hormel, Armour, Swift, and Cudahy came to dominate the meat-packing industry.

In finance, which made everything else possible, the name of John Pierpont Morgan led all the rest.

Tinkerers and inventors

Until relatively recent times, the United States has produced few men who may be called pure scientists. Of the 18 men whose likenesses were originally chosen to adorn the Washington headquarters of our National Academy of Sciences, only two were Americans—Josiah Willard Gibbs, who was professor of mathematical physics at Yale for 30 years, and Benjamin Franklin. The leisure and intellectual atmosphere in which original contributions to theoretical physics, chemistry, or biology are most often produced were absent in the hustling, bustling, still-to-be-built America of the 18th and 19th centuries. Its people were too busy laying railroad track, mining gold, sinking oil wells, and building steel mills to give much thought to theories.

But tinkering, inventing, and figuring out how things work and how to make them work better—that is something else again. With men of this turn of mind the Republic has been richly blessed. The young immigrant Samuel Slater, memorizing the plans for an entire English cotton-spinning mill and reproducing it in alien Rhode Island; Robert Fulton working to perfect his steamboat; Eli Whitney visiting a Southern cotton plantation and figuring out how to separate the seeds from the fiber; Samuel Colt devising a revolver with interchangeable parts—all these men and their achievements are familiar stories of the pre-Civil War era.

The war greatly stimulated that inventive spirit, and the industrial expansion that followed brought it to full flower. Americans got a chance to see two of the most important men of the period—although they paid them little attention at first—at the Philadelphia Centennial Exposition of 1876. In a small booth in the Machinery Hall, a young Scot named Alexander Graham Bell was exhibiting a new-fangled gadget he called a telephone. "My God!" exclaimed the visiting emperor of Brazil when he heard Bell's voice over the wire. "It talks." The other important exhibitor was Thomas Alva Edison, a 29-year-old "tramp" telegrapher who had already improved the stock ticker and the telegraph and invented wax wrapping paper and the mimeograph machine.

If any one man symbolizes the American spirit of invention, surely it is Edison, "The Wizard of Menlo Park." On an estate in that New Jersey town, he set up during the centennial year a shop whose motto was "Inventions To Order." Throughout the next half-century, there were to pour forth from his fertile imagination a dozen devices that would profoundly alter the lives of all who came after him—the first commercially practical incandescent light bulb, the electric generator, the phonograph, important contributions to the movie

"THE BEST IN THE MARKET."

Chicago's Union Stockyards in 1866 (below) used to ship livestock to local dealers until Gustavus Swift in 1875 began slaughtering animals in the yards and shipping the meat, as advertised in a meat packer's poster above.

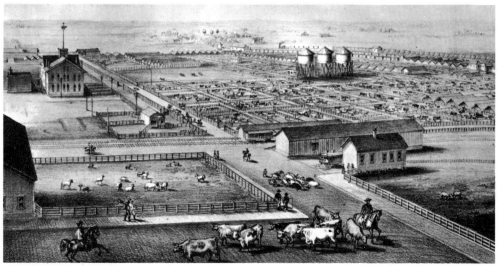

Steel mills along the Monongahela, one of the three rivers flowing through Pittsburgh, were painted by the primitive Pennsylvania artist John Kane.

industry. In his lifetime, he was granted 1,093 patents, more than any other man in American history. Progress, he had reason to know, is as much the product of persistence as of pure genius: To develop a durable filament for his incandescent bulb, he tried coconut fibers, lampwick, and hairs taken from a friend's beard before finally hitting upon a thread of carbonized paper. "There's a better way to do it," he repeatedly told the young men who worked for him. "Find it!"

In those years between Lincoln and McKinley, other persistent, inventive young men were tinkering with gadgets that were to make the achievements of the masters of industry possible. Carnegie himself backed T. T. Woodruff, who created a railroad sleeping car. After they pooled their resources with George M. Pullman, long-distance passenger travel by rail became bearable. In 1869, George Westinghouse received a patent on a railroad air brake. Previously, the brakes of each car of a train had to be operated separately; with the air brake, an engineer sitting in his cab could slow a long string of freight or passenger cars to a smooth stop. Westinghouse's brake, along with his electrical signal-control system, made the high-speed trains of Hill and Vanderbilt manageable and safe.

Later, with the help of Hungarian-born Nikola Tesla and in competition with Edison, Westinghouse would develop a practical means of supplying electric current to homes, cities, and industries. This revolutionary source of light and power was to become so essential to modern society that in 1931, when Edison died and someone proposed that all of America's electric lights and power be turned off for a moment or two in his honor, President Hoover was obliged to reject the idea. The result would have been chaos.

Arteries of steel

Enterprising leadership, inventive genius, rich resources, and a sympathetic government helped bring the industrial era to birth, but without one more factor it would never have got beyond the nursery. This was the iron horse.

So important was the spread of rail transportation that the decades after the Civil War have often been called the railroad era. Service east of the Mississippi was expanded and im-proved, but the most dramatic growth took place in the West. From 35,000 miles of road in operation in 1865, the network of tracks across the country grew to 258,000 miles before 1900.

The so-called transcontinentals attracted much attention—especially the first one, built jointly by the Union Pacific and the Central Pacific. After 1869, when the Union Pacific and the Central Pacific met at Promontory Summit in Utah, lines streaked westward. By 1870, the Kansas Pacific reached Denver. During the next 20 years, the Southern Pacific, the Atchison, Topeka & Santa Fe, the Northern Pacific, and the Great Northern all made West Coast connections.

The growth of the early railroad industry was, in a peculiarly American way, a romance. But that growth was American in another sense, too: It was marked by great speed and waste. In 1862, to encourage construction across the Great American Desert, the federal government offered every other section of a 10-mile-square tract of land for every mile of road built. Two years later, when this proved not attractive enough, the offer was doubled. Eventually, railroads received from state and federal governments a total of 155,504,994 acres—an area almost the size of Texas. In addition, extensive loans were made available. Government extravagance and mismanagement led to corruption. The Credit Mobilier, a financial organization associated with the Union Pacific, made over $50,000,000 before the road was completed—one of the many scandals that rocked the Grant administration.

Despite the hastiness and inefficiency of their construction, the roads when completed were much in demand, and invariably they made a heavy contribution to the areas they served. They opened new and fertile sections of the American West, while older parts of America, bypassed in the westward rush, emerged from their isolation only when linked to the new commercial centers.

The new age of steel was characterized by specialization. As modern transportation and communication facilities opened up new markets, manufacturers began to concentrate on a single kind of product. With specialization came interchangeability of parts, mass production, and mass marketing—all of which increased efficiency of operation. By using time-saving and laborsaving techniques and by perfecting distribution methods, the most progressive manufacturers drastically cut their unit costs. Sometimes they passed on the saving to the customers, but more often they used the profit to combine and expand in their own field, hoping to drive out competitors and thereby enlarge their own markets.

For the tendency toward consolidation and monopoly was strong during the 19th century. It was a roughhouse game in which weaker players were

SMITHSONIAN INSTITUTION

This telephone receiver is one of several that were exhibited and demonstrated by Alexander Graham Bell at the Philadelphia Exposition of 1876.

Thomas Edison had worked for 72 consecutive hours on his wax-cylinder phonograph when the photo was taken in 1888 from which this likeness was painted.

carried off the field with alarming frequency. The winners made no apologies. With some justification, they argued that the nation was the chief beneficiary of their efficiency, which brought inexpensive goods of high quality to the average household. They added that the evils of monopoly —if, indeed, there were evils—were a small price to pay for such material advancements. And it was perfectly true that their success, whatever its less desirable by-products, was due primarily to the application of initiative in a system of free enterprise. It was, therefore, quite within the American tradition.

The results were spectacular. Giant industries sprouted, reaching heights of productivity that amazed the world and made Americans proud. The genius of the Yankee inventor and the semihumorous slogan "The difficult we do at once; the impossible takes a little longer" became a part of the American heritage. The conviction spread that in this land of "go-ahead," the industrial horn of plenty would ever refill itself. The nation was confident, cocky. It had found the

He will travel, in order to compare his own condition with that of the European workingman.

Doubtless he will employ s[...] leisure in writing essays on the [...] of things in general.

When two hours is a day's work, with three holidays every week, he will have to take plenty of exercise, to keep in good physical condition.

He will elect himself to Congress, and look after his condition there, personally.

And, of course, by that time, everything will be in such a condition that Fashionable Society will welcome him with open arms.

THE AMERICAN WORKINGMAN OF THE FUTURE.
When the Labor Agitators Have "Improved His Condition" Until He is Perfectly Satisfied With It.

In 1887, Puck *ridiculed the unions for trying to improve the lot of the workingman, showing him in exaggerated situations for which he is unprepared.*

key to industrial success; ahead lay economic paradise.

Two important things were wrong with the picture, however. First, the government machinery—federal, state, and local—of a traditionally agrarian nation was not geared to cope with the problems of an industrial society. *Laissez faire,* or "let alone," was still the guiding principle.

Government, it was believed, should stand in the background—an idle policeman awaiting a report of some lawbreaking before taking action.

The second trouble lay in the distribution system. All too often, manufactured goods failed to get into the hands of the intended users, and foodstuffs did not find their way from the farm to the hungry city workers.

There were enough railroads, warehouses, and telephone and telegraph facilities to keep the goods moving, but as the 19th century got older, the nation seemed to be suffering from a hardening of the economic arteries. To businessmen, whose capacity to understand the complexities of distribution had been outstripped by the speed of their country's commercial growth, the causes of the ailment were a mystery. Still, they were quick to object to suggestions that the federal government step in and try to effect a cure. There was, they believed, no cause for concern. As for the government, without major changes it was in no position to play such a part.

There were other troubles. From time to time, industry overproduced —or, as the manufacturers preferred to say—the nation underconsumed. Whichever it was, the results were industrial cramps and spasms. An unfavorable market almost always caused a shutdown of factories until demand picked up again. This brought extreme hardship to the workers, crowded as they were into their industrial ghettos.

Still, for a long time, ordinary people—like the tycoons themselves—did not want to go to any great length in search of a remedy. Few, rich or poor, questioned the theory that there was opportunity for all. With achievement measured in dollars, no one thought of condemning the Carnegies, the Rockefellers, or the Morgans; they were simply ordinary men who had gained fortune's favor. The common man felt that in this marvelous national lottery, his might be the next name called out.

The Robber Barons

The trouble with American financial success was that it was sometimes too successful. Ex-Ambassador Charles Francis Adams, returning from England in 1871, complained that the first five years after Appomattox "witnessed some of the most remarkable examples of organized lawlessness, under the forms of law, which mankind had yet had an opportunity to study." It struck him as wrong that one man could command hundreds of miles of railroads and another could have hundreds of millions of dollars. "In all this they have wielded a practical independence of control of both governments and of individuals," he wrote. By the end of the century, a great many Americans had begun, however unconsciously, to agree with him. To them, wealth was one thing, but excessive wealth seemed to warrant investigation. When money began to affect political developments or tilt the scales of justice, something had to be done.

But what? Opinions varied. A few reformers were ready to scrap capitalism; others, mainly the socialists, talked about major revisions. At the other extreme were men of means like Andrew Carnegie, who, seeing no reason for change at all, continued to preach the gospel of "work and save."

The system was right; if men did not become millionaires, the cause lay in something other than a deficiency in the system itself.

That argument did not satisfy all Americans. There appeared, late in the 19th century, an increasing amount of literature critical of capitalism—Edward Bellamy's novel *Looking Backward;* Henry George's immensely popular *Progress and Poverty;* Henry Demerest Lloyd's *Wealth Against Commonwealth.* To the distress of the wealthy, what a later age would call their public image was beginning to deteriorate. Some of them tried to ignore the talk. Others, disturbed by the insinuation that they were simply taking what they wanted, eased their consciences by giving it away. But most agreed that the outcries against them and capitalism were subversive.

Those who demanded that big business be regulated did not consider themselves subversive. They went on the theory that monopoly could be efficient but at the same time harmful to consumers. The emergence of trusts controlling large segments of the economy was of particular concern. Standard Oil, for example, accounted for 90% of the petroleum industry; the American Sugar Refining Company, about 85% of the sugar industry.

In answer to growing complaints, Congress, in 1890, passed the Sherman Antitrust Act prohibiting "combinations . . . in restraint of trade." It was loosely drawn: Nowhere did it define a trust or explain what restraint of trade meant. Senator Orville Platt of Connecticut frankly admitted, "The conduct of the Senate has not been in the line of honest preparation of a bill to prohibit and punish trusts . . . and the whole effort has been to get some bill headed 'A Bill To Punish Trusts' with which to go to the country." The truth of the Senator's statement was revealed during the 1890s, when the Supreme Court handed down decision after decision against those trying to enforce the law. Initially, most of the actual prosecutions were directed against labor unions—considered, in a business-minded society, "combinations" restraining trade. Thus, although the Sherman Act was intended to protect the laborer and the consumer from monopolistic power, it was for many years exercised for the opposite end.

Robber Barons on the defensive

Nevertheless, the industrialists did not go unregulated throughout the age of steel. Indeed, the Civil War was not many years past before they were stung by regulatory or tax laws passed by individual state legislatures. For relief, business quickly turned to the Supreme Court, traditionally conservative and always jealous of legislative powers. The immediate weapon used by corporation lawyers was that clause of the Fourteenth Amendment that says no state shall "deprive any person of life, liberty, or property, without due process of law." It was one of the reconstruction-era amendments, and most people assumed that the "person" referred to was the American Negro. Businessmen insisted, however, that a corporation was an entity, hence an individual or a person, and that the various states, through excessive taxation and regulation, were trying to take corporate property without due process.

At first, the courts upheld the state legislatures, but after about 15 years of trying, the corporations won their first big case before the high court: In the Minnesota Rate Case of 1889, the justices agreed that the action of a state legislature to reduce rail rates constituted a deprivation of property without due process. That broke the dam. During the next three decades, the Fourteenth Amendment was used nearly 800 times to protect corporations against hamstringing legislation.

Labor flexes its muscles

As society became more and more industrialized, business faced another challenge—organized labor, which wanted better working conditions and a larger share of the profits. Before the Civil War, nationwide labor unions had been almost nonexistent, and in the immediate postwar years, labor made scant progress. It had little power to enforce its demands.

When organized workers finally turned militant, employers called for

Eugene Debs and his American Railway Union were considered by the artist a threat to the nation's economy because of their strike for higher wages.

Federal cavalry clears the way for a train to pass through the American Railway Union's lines in Chicago, Illinois, during the Pullman strike that took place in June, 1894.

help, and it came—in the form of state or federal troops. But hard times, touched off by the panic of 1873, put workers in a fighting mood. By 1877, there were a number of strikes, principally against the railroads. Both the Baltimore & Ohio and the Pennsylvania were struck that year, and in both cases federal bayonets—provided by President Rutherford B. Hayes—were used to break up the rioting. The trouble spread to the Delaware, Lackawanna & Western, and as far west as Chicago.

The strikes of 1877 gained little for the railroad workers, but in the long view they benefited labor as a whole by demonstrating that it had fighting power. The Knights of Labor, founded in 1869, now took on new strength and prepared for future battles. By the middle 1880s, the Knights had 700,-000 members.

Then came trouble. A series of unsuccessful strikes discouraged a good many members, and in the spring of 1886, the violence erupted that was to put the whole labor movement, and the Knights in particular, in bad repute.

In May, a long strike against the McCormick Harvesting Machine Company in Chicago resulted in a riot. Police broke it up, and in Haymarket Square the next day, when workers returned to protest, someone threw a bomb that killed seven persons and injured 60 more. Although no one could positively identify the bomb thrower, a judge found eight "anarchists" guilty and sentenced seven of them to death. Four of the condemned were hanged, one committed suicide, and the other two had their sentences commuted to life imprisonment. Although the Knights of Labor were in no way responsible for the riot or its consequences, labor in general suffered, and the Knights ex-

perienced a serious decline. By 1890, their membership had dwindled to about 100,000.

Out of the wreckage of the Knights there arose the American Federation of Labor, led by Samuel Gompers, a member of Local No. 144 of the Cigar Makers' Union of New York City. The new organization was composed of a number of craft unions combined into one large federation, with a structure resembling that of the United States government. Each member un-

ion had complete power to deal with its employers, the federation itself merely acting as a national representative and co-ordinator.

Among the battles fought by the A.F.L., two stand out. The first was waged in 1892 in the Homestead, Pennsylvania, plant of the Carnegie Steel Company. There, some 300 Pinkerton detectives were hired to evict the strikers. The steelworkers fired upon the Pinkertons as they sailed up the Monongahela River toward the

829

plant. After a wild affray, the strike-breakers surrendered, were held prisoners of war for 24 hours, and then were run out of town. Henry Frick, in charge of Carnegie's operations at the time, called for help and promptly received it in the form of soldiers. Management broke the strike.

The second conflict grew out of a dispute between sleeping-car manufacturer George M. Pullman and his employees in the factory town of Pullman, Illinois. In 1894, management cut wages but continued to charge the same food prices at the company stores and the same rents for company houses. The American Railway Union under Eugene V. Debs came to the aid of the Pullman workers, and the disorder spread to all Western railroads using the company's cars. The railroads made management's familiar plea for federal assistance, and President Grover Cleveland gave it, over the heated protests of Governor John P. Altgeld of Illinois. It was another triumph for the industrialists, who knew that they had behind them a large body of American opinion and hence the administration at Washington, whether Democratic or Republican. It is small wonder that the supporters of organized labor found their uphill fight discouraging.

Modern America

Toward the end of the 19th century, a new American nation emerged—one whose characteristics sufficiently resembled those of the present day to be called "modern." Not only did manufacturers supply those who went forth to conquer what remained of the unsettled West, but they looked around the globe for new markets. It was a time of great urban growth, of a steady movement of people from the farm to the city. It was also a time when a man with real ability and a little luck could, as the popular Horatio Alger used to put it, "rise from the ranks" to great power and wealth. For thousands of young Americans who aspired to follow them up the ladder, the success of Carnegie, Rockefeller, and Morgan was a spine-tingling story.

But it was not written without a price. In the wild scramble to the top, some allowed their acquisitive instincts to dominate everything else, and the world came to think of all Americans as dollar chasers. In that chase there were many innocent casualties. Men worked at such a pace that health was endangered. Industrial slums proliferated. The end in sight was wealth, and the means became secondary.

By 1900, thoughtful persons had begun to look upon the warfare among the business titans with growing distaste. Angered by what they considered the apathy of most of their fellow citizens, a few of these men and women resolved to spread the gospel of reform. Their success paralleled David's victory over Goliath. But that story belongs to another era of history.

COVERDALE AND COLPITTS

MAKE WAY FOR THE IRON HORSE!

In 1804, when canal boat and stagecoach were the accepted modes of travel, an Englishman built the world's first successful locomotive. Puffing at five miles an hour along a nine-mile track, it carried ore for an ironworks in Wales. By 1830, the idea had crossed the Atlantic, and a locomotive built in New York made the first passenger run in the United States. It could pull 50 passengers at 21 miles an hour. Canal and stagecoach men saw the handwriting on the wall: despite their dire warnings of exploding boilers on these steam monsters, the public took to the new contraption, and by the beginning of the Civil War, the nation had 31,246 miles of railroads. In addition, it had a new hero for the American boy—the brave engineer standing at the throttle of the *Fast Mail* as it thundered past, smoke belching and brass gleaming, with its hook out to seize the mail pouch (above).

MAKE WAY FOR THE IRON HORSE!

FROM COAST TO COAST

Inevitably, the demand arose for a coast-to-coast rail system. In 1862, Lincoln signed the Pacific Railroad Act, and two new companies were formed to undertake the construction job. The Central Pacific (above) started at Sacramento, and with a labor force made up largely of Chinese laborers, pushed east over the Rockies. The Union Pacific was to begin with existing railheads at Omaha and drive west. At last the great day came (right) when the two lines tied the country together.

THE DRIVING
OF THE
GOLDEN SPIKE

The Civil War had created a labor shortage, so the Union Pacific made up the deficit by importing workmen from Ireland. As the two lines drew closer, friction grew between Irish and Chinese, and there were a number of brawls. In spite of them, the two lines were finally linked on May 10, 1869, at Promontory Summit, Utah. Assorted dignitaries were to drive the golden spike that made the final link, but the gentlemen could not handle a sledge hammer, and that job was done by a Union Pacific construction boss. The photograph (right) shows the actual event; the painting (above) is a fiction commissioned by Governor Leland Stanford of California, which shows the governor himself standing in the center of the tracks. Some of the others were not even alive.

THE ROADS GROW UP

The story of post-Civil War railroading is the story of little lines, some of which operated fewer than 100 miles of track, being absorbed into larger and more efficient systems. As the lines fought for business with blaring posters, big roads swallowed little ones and then fought among themselves until the biggest, like Cornelius Vanderbilt's New York Central, had acquired huge holdings.

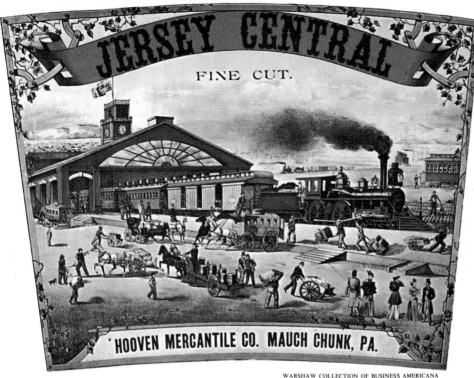

JERSEY CENTRAL
FINE CUT.

HOOVEN MERCANTILE CO. MAUCH CHUNK, PA.

TRAMP! TRAMP!! TRAMP!!!
THE BOYS ARE MARCHING ON TO
VIA THE DENVER
GREAT Rock Island
ROUTE

TO THE
REUNION
OF THE
GRAND ARMY REPUBLIC
JULY 24TH & 28TH 1883

FROM CHICAGO, PEORIA, ROCK ISLAND, KEOKUK OR OTTUMWA,
With Choice of Four Routes from the Missouri River, via Council Bluffs, Kansas City, Leavenworth or Atchison.
FOR FURTHER INFORMATION, CALL UPON OR ADDRESS

RAPID TRANSIT
SAVE TIME TAKE THE A DISTANCE
HOOSAC TUNNEL ROUTE
HOOSAC
1875

SHORTEST LINE BETWEEN CARRYING THE UNITED STATES MAIL
THE EAST AND WEST
CONNECTING WITH THE
NEW YORK CENTRAL R.R.
GENERAL OFFICE, 250 Washington St. BOSTON.

837

TROUBLE
IN THE WEST

On the frontier, harsher perils than predatory financiers faced the railroads. Prairie fires might threaten the cars, and the still plentiful buffalo (above) could derail a train if stampeded. The Indians (below) did not care for the iron horse on their hunting grounds, and passengers often used their own firearms while waiting for the United States cavalry to come riding to the rescue.

COLLECTION OF A. HOWARD STEBBINS

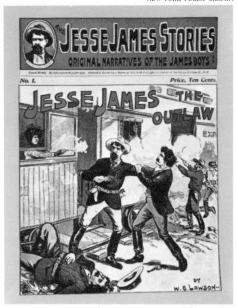

An even more serious threat than Indians was that posed by train robbers, whose crimes reached a peak in the 1870s. The James gang (below, seated, left to right, are Frank and Jesse; standing, cohorts Cole and Bob Younger) virtually became national heroes (right), with deeds celebrated in the Robin Hood tradition. Sympathy for the James boys was rife among small farmers, whose anger was directed against the railroads for charging them higher rates than the bigger shippers paid. In the end, the train robbers were recognized for what they were—common gunmen—and farmers turned to peaceable organizations like the Grange to put their plight before Congress.

RIDING ON THE ROADS

Railroad travel had come a long way from the bare wooden benches on which the early passengers had jolted. In 1864, the enterprising George Pullman began building his Pullman Palace Car (right) that even included comfortable sleeping accommodations. The station lunch counter (below) was replaced by the dining car, and trips became so safe that small children traveled alone (below, right). The very wealthy were transported in their own richly appointed private cars. The Pullman company produced at least 350 of these.

MAKE WAY FOR THE IRON HORSE!

THE HEYDAY OF THE HORSE

In the railroads' great days, the arrival of a train was a high point in the life of a town. Above, in the painting by E. L. Henry, the 9:45 a.m. *Accommodation* has just pulled into Stratford, Connecticut. The engine is a wood burner, as one can tell from the "balloon" smokestack; the engineer has decorated the headlight with a pair of antlers. The town has come to say goodbys, to meet arrivals, and simply to take a look at their most important link with the world.

CHAPTER 29

AGRICULTURE, ADVERSITY, AND AGITATION

America has often been called the promised land. The promise is made up of many things: Political freedom, for one. Religious toleration, for another. And, of course, the opportunity for each man to follow his private dream and rise as high as his abilities will take him. But present-day Americans, especially those who are city-bred, may find it hard to realize how important a part of the promise was land itself. To an impoverished European peasant destined to live out his life tilling the soil of a wealthy landlord, or even to a New England farmer trying to scratch a livelihood out of a rocky hillside pasture, the rich and almost unbelievably abundant land west of the Mississippi seemed paradise indeed.

And it was so easy to own. Beginning with the Ordinance of 1785 and extending to the Homestead Act of 1862, the acquisition of farm sites steadily became easier. The Preemption Act of 1841 set the price of public land at $1.25 an acre and con-

The slogan under the main figure in this granger poster, "I Pay for All," gives the farmer's view of his place in the economy.

ferred upon the buyer the right to plant a crop and build a cabin on it even before it had been surveyed. Then, with the passage of the Homestead Act, any citizen could obtain a quarter section—160 acres—merely by paying nominal filing charges and living on it for five years. The words "free land" had a powerful effect upon prospective settlers: At the end of the Civil War, thousands of former soldiers and even greater numbers of nonveterans moved across the Missouri River to seek out new homes on the plains.

But 160 acres was not enough, particularly if the farmer also wanted to graze cattle on it. In 1877, Congress passed the Desert Land Act, offering homesteaders an additional section (640 acres) in exchange for a 25¢-an-acre filing fee and "conducting water upon the land." Buyers had three years to "prove up." Many stockmen, however, abused the government's generosity. They bought thousands of acres by means of a simple subterfuge: They put their cattle to graze on it for three years and told their cowboys to sprinkle a cupful of water here and there so the land would be "irrigated."

The wooded areas of the West Coast became the lumberman's paradise after passage of the 1878 Timber and Stone Act, under which land was sold cheaply.

Sometimes they carried the pretense further and put in some "ditches," but these were no more than plow furrows that ran up and down hills with no regard to the laws of gravity. Then, instead of proving up, the stockmen simply sold their land at a considerable profit to the first interested buyers.

Another government attempt to give away more land—although it did not help farmers much—was the Timber and Stone Act of 1878, under which a man could buy, for as little as $2.50 an acre, quarter sections of wooded, rocky land unfit for cultivation. West Coast lumbermen scoured the grogshops for hangers-on who would register their claims and then turn them over to the companies for logging. At first, the fee for such a service was $50, but soon it dropped until men could be found who would oblige for a glass of beer. By the 20th century, over 3,500,000 acres of valuable forest land were taken up under the law. But despite the fraudulent activities of stockmen and lumber interests, the settlement of the West by individual farmers went on.

The government, by repeatedly liberalizing the Homestead Act, set off the greatest land rush in the history of the country. The movement was so great during the 1870s that even the Mississippi Valley states lost population to the adjoining plains. This army of native settlers was joined by millions of immigrants, who, to claim land, needed only to declare their intention of becoming citizens.

Within a decade after the Civil War, some Easterners began to fear that the movement was too large and too fast.

No one listened to them. Even though the panic of 1873 had driven agricultural prices down 10% to 30%, the westward movement persisted. Free government land, or cheap railroad land, still was available in quantity. Hard times and savage competition had kept most railroad rates from rising and had even lowered some of them. The European markets still demanded grain in quantity. Money could still be made behind a plow.

Technological advances also sustained the migration westward. Improvements and recent inventions in farm machinery meant that more land could be worked by the average fam-

Two cowboys, in this painting by Charles Russell titled Come Out of There, *try to rope a stray cow that has wandered off with its calf down a gully.*

ily unit. Cyrus McCormick's reaper and John Deere's steel plow had been in general use since the Civil War, of course, but now, to join them in making life on the farm easier, came a rush of useful machines. Within a single President's term, that of Rutherford B. Hayes (1876–1880), the spring-tooth harrow, the twine binder, the centrifugal cream separator, and the gang plow were developed, and within a decade after that, Iowa corn growers were shucking and binding their crop mechanically. Cheaper land and laborsaving devices had a dramatic effect. In the last three decades of the century, the number of acres under cultivation jumped from fewer than 500,000,000 to nearly 900,000,000. In the aggregate, farming was becoming big business.

Advances in milling methods also helped. In an earlier day, flour made from the hard kernels of spring wheat had been of low quality. Then came the invention of the roller process that successfully milled spring wheat—the hard, high-protein grain that grew

Pulled by 33 horses, this combine heads, threshes, and cleans the grain as it moves across a wheat field near Walla Walla, Washington, in 1902.

This homesteader is foraging ahead of his wagon, and with one bird in hand, he stands ready for whatever else might flush from the deep grass.

best across the northern part of the United States. Farmers poured into Minnesota, the Dakotas, and later, Montana. The nation's per-capita production of grain nearly doubled between 1860 and 1880, and America's milling capital moved westward from Rochester, New York, to Minneapolis.

The Western railroads were a tremendous stimulus to settlement. In this new age of steel, the old iron tracks gave way to heavier rails, and such advances as the Westinghouse air brake made trains out of what had once been unwieldy strings of cars. The result was a greater carrying capacity and higher speeds for the

railroads, which soon began to penetrate virgin country.

Building in advance of settlement, laying down numerous feeders, or granger roads, the railroads beckoned the farmers westward and helped persuade them to stay by guaranteeing swift and efficient delivery of any and all crops they could grow.

It was an aggressive campaign. In thousands of newspaper advertisements, pamphlets, posters, and brochures, the railroads touted the new promised land. Papers as far away as Norway, Sweden, and Germany told how easily land could be had in the American West. In its first year, the Northern Pacific immigration bu-

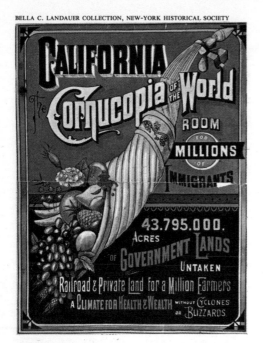

A poster designed to draw settlers to the State of California told of free land and opportunity, pointing out, at the end, that there were no cyclones or blizzards.

reau, established in 1874, sent out 25,-000 circulars and 25,000 booklets—one-fifth of them printed in German. By 1883, the Northern Pacific had 800 agents operating in the United Kingdom, 20 in London alone. Inquiries from would-be immigrants soared to 60,000 a year, and in reply over 2,500,000 pieces of literature were mailed.

Such literature painted the American West in glowing terms. Seed, it was said, produced crops of amazing size. Drought, loneliness, and Indians—the major enemies of the pioneer homesteader—were discreetly unmentioned. In an exaggerated passage, the Union Pacific praised the Platte

Valley as "a flowery meadow of great fertility clothed in nutritious grasses, and watered by numerous streams." According to Burlington Railroad pamphlets, Western wheat farms produced 30 bushels to the acre, and cornfields 70 bushels. Crop samples and testimonial letters were sent to all parts of the world. Here was concrete evidence of a plowman's utopia, waiting only for the plow.

Growing pains

Free land, cheap transportation, and powerfully persuasive railroad advertising—all these helped flood the West with farmers. Although the land did not in every case live up to advance billing, it did in the aggregate yield more grain than America or Europe was prepared to eat. These enormous American crops, combined with mounting agricultural competition from Russia, Canada, Australia, and Argentina, glutted the world market and drove prices down. Corn that commanded 63¢ a bushel in this country during 1881 sold for only 28¢ in 1890. That year out in Kansas (where transportation charges had to be deducted), it was worth a mere 10¢ a bushel. During the 1880s, wheat averaged just above 70¢ a bushel, and the price of cotton had plummeted from 15¢ a pound to 8¢. Conditions became so bad that a Nebraska farmer was said to have shot his hogs, for he could neither sell them nor give them away. His plight seemed to support the national statistics; farming was losing out as a means of livelihood.

Why? The easy and apparently obvious explanation was overproduction. But that was hard for any farmer to understand. From the time of the first settlements, there had been—except for seasonal transportation stoppages—a steady market for farm produce. Despite the tremendous increase in crop production after the Civil War, there still were Easterners who did not have all the food they needed. As long as makers of clothes were underfed and producers of food were underclad, farmers believed that the term "overproduction" was meaningless. Quite reasonably they asked why Kansans were burning corn for fuel when laborers along the Atlantic seaboard were in need of groceries. They wondered if there were not some artificial barrier between producer and consumer. Were there not "certain influences at work, like thieves in

Immigrants traveling to their new homes in the West set up housekeeping and often spent their long and hard journey in a single railway coach.

the night," bent upon robbing the farmer of his labors? It seemed there were: The railroads.

Robber Barons on rails

The reputation of the Western roads fluctuated violently. When they had plunged across unsettled country, gambling that enough farmers would follow in their wake to make transportation profitable, they had been the darlings of the Western public. Their fabulously low rates, offered to farmers who wished to move their entire families onto a homestead, and even to excursionists who merely wanted to look over the Western farm lands, brought the warmest approval. Of course, all the time the railroads were receiving large land grants for laying tracks across the trans-Mississippi West, but the farmer did not begrudge them that privilege until he himself was faced with poverty and bankruptcy. Then he turned against the railroads and blamed them for his problems, just as he had blamed the Second Bank of the United States half a century earlier. The West's railroaders now became its villains.

When these corporate giants warred upon one another and lowered rates in competitive areas, they were inclined to recoup resultant losses by charging more in other Western areas where they had a monopoly. Overnight these new benefactors became criminals in the eyes of their agricultural customers. Some crops had to be moved as many as 2,000 miles to market, and the railroads did not try to hide the fact that they were charging all the traffic would bear. Angered farmers complained that when it cost one bushel of corn to send another bushel to market, it was more than they could afford.

To be fair, many of the roads were in a precarious financial position. Often they had been conceived in the belief that the creation of towns along the route and the resultant increase in the value of adjacent railroad lands would bring handsome profits. The towns themselves had become great railroad boosters. In the 1880s, one small Kansas town that served as headquarters for one road and was located on the principal route of another, voted bonds for still a third, tried to get a fourth to include it on its route, and appointed committees to search for still more roads.

In a good many instances this kind of promotion failed to bring the railroads the profits they had expected. Faced by declining revenues, their officials saw no recourse but to continue high rates. The farmers had no choice but to pay. Shippers complained, loudly, too, that short-haul rates were much higher than those for the long haul. It was hard for them to understand why, in the words of historian John D. Hicks, "wheat could actually be sent from Chicago to Liverpool for less than from certain points in Dakota to the Twin Cities."

Similarly, Dakota wheat growers were furious because they were re-

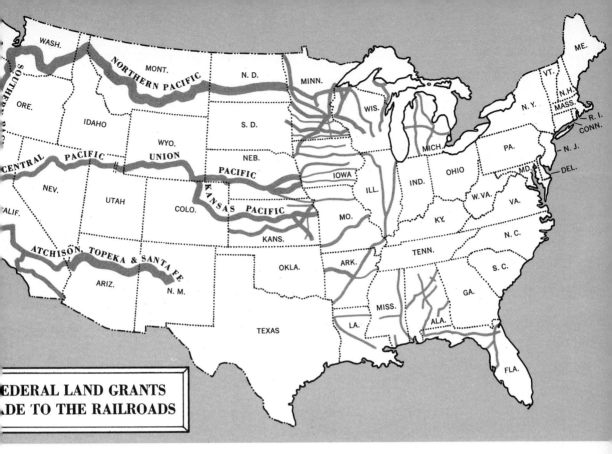

Approximate areas of federal land grants to the railroads are shown by the dark lines on the map. Part of the cost of building these railroads was met by selling some of this land to farmers who came to settle there.

quired to use railroad-owned elevators, where both loading and storage charges were assessed. To make matters even worse, elevator managers had a habit of "downgrading"—arbitrarily classifying the wheat as being of a lower grade, so they could buy it cheaper. The farmer was helpless. He could submit, or he could take his wheat home. As a rule he sold, but every time he did, his bitterness grew.

Prairie politics

Americans are a peaceful people, but if they are pushed around—or feel that they are being pushed around—they will get up and fight. In the latter years of the 19th century, this is exactly what farmers did.

During the 1870s, they rallied to the banner of the Patrons of Husbandry, organized in 1867 by a Bureau of Agriculture clerk named Oliver H. Kelley. By 1875, the Patrons had 800,-000 members in 20,000 granges, or local units. The Patrons organized hundreds of granger cooperatives, elevators, creameries, and warehouses, started farm-machinery factories, set up insurance companies for their membership, and originated the mail-order business—which, after Montgomery Ward was founded in 1872, would pass into other hands. All

853

The classroom of the schoolhouse in Edwardsville, Illinois, is used in the early 1870s by the local grange to hold its meetings and discussions.

these projects were aimed at lowering prices for the farmers, but this did not reach the root of their difficulty. A good many of them were still frustrated by the attitude of the courts and disappointed that the political power of the Grange was not greater or its representatives more aggressive. They were in an angry mood and wanted a fighting leadership.

In the National Farmers' Alliance, organized in 1877, they hoped they had the answer. Its main objectives were to seek more favorable railroad and tax legislation and to legalize Grange insurance companies. The father of the Alliance was Milton George, editor of the *Western Rural,*

a Chicago farm journal. Hard times during the early 1880s stimulated the movement and sharpened George's accusations against the railroads. By 1882, the Alliance was said to have 100,000 members; by 1890, hard times were so general in the rural West that over 1,000 new members were joining each week.

The local chapters of the Alliance made their presence felt. They were loud in their agitation for state regulation—if not outright ownership—of corporations, and they openly opposed absentee ownership of rural land. They demanded the establishment of agricultural subtreasuries—government warehouses where farmers could store their nonperishable products, receiving loans of up to 80% of the market value while holding their crops for more favorable prices. Within a single lifetime, this would no longer be considered a wild-eyed scheme. In the administrations of Woodrow Wilson and Franklin D. Roosevelt it would become reality.

Perhaps the most important political movement of the late '80s was the People's Party, commonly called the Populists. It was first organized in Kansas during the spring of 1890, and during the next two years, membership skyrocketed. By February of 1892, a national organization was formed. The views of the National Farmers' Alliance, if not its membership, became thoroughly identified with the new party. By campaign time in 1892, the agrarians were strong enough to enter national politics, and they did so with much fanfare.

At their first national nominating convention, held at Omaha, Nebraska,

With Carl Browne leading the parade on horseback, part of Jacob S. Coxey's army marches to Washington in 1894 to seek an end to unemployment.

that summer, the Populists made General James B. Weaver of Iowa their candidate for President. An able man, he had run for the Presidency on the Greenback ticket in 1880 and was fairly well known. An equally good choice as his running mate was ex-Confederate General James G. Field of Virginia. Former army officers like Grant, Hayes, and Garfield had dominated the Presidency since the Civil War, and the Populists hoped that a ticket with two of them—one from the North and one from the South—would have wide appeal.

The Populists declare themselves

The Populists' platform called for the free and unlimited coinage of silver, the adoption of the Alliance's subtreasury scheme, a graduated income tax, a postal savings bank, land reform, and government ownership of railroad, telegraph, and telephone facilities. They also asked for immigration restrictions and a shorter working day for industrial laborers. In an attempt to keep the party machinery out of the hands of professional politicians, the Populists approved a rule stating that no person holding a municipal, state, or federal office could sit or vote at any Populist convention. Many people vigorously approved.

The campaign of 1892 was more interesting and colorful than any had been for a long time. The Populists' major candidates made their appeal largely to the agricultural South and West, trying to acquire enough political power to exercise a balance of control between the two older, traditional parties. Outspoken characters such as "Sockless Jerry" Simpson, Mary Elizabeth Lease, and Minnesota firebrand Ignatius Donnelly attracted wide attention. Mrs. Lease's advice to Kansas farmers to "raise less corn and more hell" was one of the memorable remarks of the campaign.

Thoroughly aroused, the Populists went to the polls in November, fiercely determined to make political history. They did. Democrat Grover Cleveland won the Presidency with 277 electoral votes to 145 for his Republican opponent, Benjamin Harrison, but Weaver polled over 1,000,000 popular votes and 22 electoral votes. His party carried Nevada, Idaho, Colorado, and Kansas; it elected governors in Colorado, Kansas, and North Dakota and sent 10 Representatives and five Senators to Washington. It was an impressive performance. Both major parties, not to mention the industrial East, could smell the smoke of this political prairie fire.

Success in 1892 generated considerable optimism among the Populists. They entered the off-year elections of 1894 with high hopes, but this time they were disappointed. Republicans recaptured Colorado and Idaho; there were reverses in Minnesota, the Dakotas, and Kansas; and in Iowa, General Weaver himself went down to defeat attempting to win a seat in the House of Representatives. But general distress brought on by the depression

GONE CRAZY.

An 1896 cartoon mocks the Democratic Party split between the sound-money men and the wild silverites, who are shown here leading the party into an abyss.

of 1893 sharpened the Populist appeal. Cleveland's attempt to stabilize the monetary situation by urging a repeal of the Sherman Silver Purchase Act produced some dark talk among Westerners. Even the Eastern businessmen, who breathed easier after the repeal, soon admitted that it had not cured

the financial ailment. Holders of silver certificates now surrendered them, but so many asked for gold in exchange that it began to appear that the government could not meet its obligations. Cleveland then made himself unpopular by borrowing gold from the banking house of J. P. Morgan. Out of the silver-producing West came cries of "betrayal" and "traitor."

The year 1894 was a time of discouragement for many Americans. Farm prices slumped to new lows and wages continued to fall. Bands of unemployed men formed themselves into "armies" led by "generals." In the spring of 1894, one of these restless groups—500 men under "General" Jacob S. Coxey—marched to Washington, where they chanted their demands outside the Capitol. The government responded by arresting the leaders for walking on the Capitol lawn.

In the West, where most farmers were always in debt, there was constant agitation that more money be put into circulation. This eventually crystallized into a demand for the free and unlimited coinage of silver at the ratio of 16 parts of silver to 1 of gold. A program of "free silver" was attractive not only to farmers but to silver miners, whose product had fallen in price. As the campaign of 1896 drew near, the "silverites" and the Populists were determined to join the "silver Democrats," in opposition to both the Republicans and the Cleveland "gold" Democrats. This political alliance would be the final attempt of the agrarians in the 19th century to gain their objectives at the polls.

At their nominating convention in 1896, the Republicans showed the

THE KEEPERS AT THE GATE.

same conservatism that, except for Cleveland's two terms, had carried them to victory ever since the Civil War. They nominated William McKinley of Ohio, best known for his protective tariff bill of 1890. In McKinley, "advance agent of prosperity," the Republicans hoped they had found a man who could stave off the Western uprising and put the Grand Old Party back in power. He and his party came out strongly for "sound money" as opposed to what they called "debased currency." Clearly the battle was to revolve around the money question.

The Democrats, divided between the gold and silver factions, bypassed

President Cleveland, the titular head of their party, and nominated silverite William Jennings Bryan, "the boy orator of the Platte." The young Nebraskan had set the convention afire with one of the greatest speeches in America's political history. Its memorable closing words were: "We will answer their demand for a gold standard by saying to them, 'You shall not press down upon the brow of labor this crown of thorns, you shall not crucify mankind upon a cross of gold.'" (See the special contribution on William Jennings Bryan at the end of this volume.)

The campaign was largely sectional. Bryan invaded the East—"enemy country," he called it—only briefly. He was more at home in the West, among his own people, and they responded to him. According to one legend, his appearance at Omaha drew such a large crowd that the auditorium overflowed. Not wishing to exclude anyone, Bryan agreed to speak outside, but the only thing he could find to stand on was a manure spreader. Without a moment's hesitation he mounted it, telling the crowd, "This is the first time I have ever spoken on a Republican platform." Earthy remarks like these had an enormous appeal to farmers, and Bryan's popularity soared.

The country had not seen such a campaign for decades and would not see anything like it again for many a year. Emotions ran especially high in the rural West. Kansas editor William Allen White compared the farmers' zeal to the fanaticism of the Crusaders. They drove their teams for miles through the night to hear pro-Bryan speakers in country schoolhouses. Bitter epithets were heaped upon Bryan in the East, and insurance companies hinted they would extend farm mortgages if McKinley were elected; but all this only strengthened the farmers' righteous resolve to vote for Bryan.

The mighty tide of rural resentment was not enough to put Bryan in the White House, however. McKinley, carrying the populous industrial states, won nearly 100 more electoral votes than the Westerner, even though the popular vote was closer—7,035,638 to 6,467,946. One Eastern religious magazine suggested the relief felt in some circles when it said, "Praise the Lord: The cause of National honor and righteousness has triumphed. The leaders of the forces of Free Silver and Repudiation, anarchy and class hatred have been overthrown, and their unrighteous cause is lost forever."

The election amply proved that the industrial world could hurl back the agrarian forces, no matter how great their anger or how solid their political organization. Westerners and Southerners had reason to be discouraged, but their children would live to see many of the Populist dreams come true when another era of hard times gave birth to Franklin D. Roosevelt's New Deal. That, however, would take a generation of waiting.

THE ROBBER BARONS

The name did not come into use until 1934, when Matthew Josephson coined it for the title of a book, but it is now part of the language. The Robber Barons were the great men of finance in late 19th-century America—famous men like the Vanderbilts, Carnegie, Morgan, and Rockefeller—but there were many other businessmen, the names of whom are not so famous, who expressed the new vitality that came into the country as the Industrial Revolution pervaded America during and after the Civil War. There was unleashed a new pioneer spirit, a certain recklessness and lawlessness, and a powerful creative talent—all centered around the single idea of accumulating as much money as possible. These men seemed to feel themselves free to operate as they wanted, the only standard being financial success. In this sense they represent better than any other single group the dynamic, imaginative, and often reckless power of the American economic system. It is to these men that part of America's economic greatness is traced. (In the cartoon, Vanderbilt, Gould, Field, and others divide the transportation profits in New York, with the suggestion that they might purchase Europe.)

861

THE VANDERBILTS

BROWN BROTHERS

CORNELIUS VANDERBILT

CULVER PICTURES

WILLIAM H. VANDERBILT

Cornelius Vanderbilt, known as the Commodore because of his control of the ferry lines around New York City, was one of the first captains of industry, but it was not until he was 68, with a fortune of $11,000,000, that he began the period of his greatest success. It was at this time that he invested in railroads, bringing into existence the great New York Central. His method was to buy a railroad, improve it without spending too much money, consolidate it with other railroads to cut expenses, increase the value of the stock (sometimes by watering), and make it pay higher dividends.

One of his most difficult financial battles was over control of the Erie Railroad. It was a fracas in which Vanderbilt faced Jay Gould and James Fisk, who had taken as their cohort Daniel Drew. The story of the Erie thrown among these rivals is one of the tricks in financial legerdemain. The ending found Gould, Fisk, and Drew in a hotel in Jersey City, New Jersey, having sold illegal stock to Vanderbilt, and the Commodore in New York, throwing out injunctions for their arrest that could not be served. Finally, in 1868, they had to come to terms with Vanderbilt, but they also received their share of stock in the Erie.

William H. Vanderbilt was the Commodore's plain, stout son, who, late in life, after being a farmer on Staten Island, surprised people by turning into a brilliant, penny-pinching president of the New York Central. His giant figure in the cartoon, with Gould and Cyrus Field on his legs, shows the control he exercised over the transportation world of New York, including even the municipal transport in which Field was involved.

THE MODERN COLOSSUS OF (RAIL) ROADS.

JAY GOULD

THE ROBBER BARONS

GOULD AND FISK

JAY GOULD'S PRIVATE BOWLING ALLEY.

864

WONDERFUL TOUR DE FORCE,

"ON THE BEACH AT LONG BRANCH," BY PROFESSOR JAMES FISK, JR. THE GREAT AMERICAN ATHLETE.

JAMES FISK

Jay Gould, silent and continually nervous, has been described as the most ruthless man on Wall Street. There was nothing about his personality to suggest that James Fisk become his partner. Fisk was a gregarious man, a loud and lavish spender. Yet he was also a sly businessman with great energy, and Gould found him a perfect foil.

One of the most incredible moves by any of the big financiers was made by Gould and Fisk in 1869 when they tried to take over the gold market of the country. The two worked with speed and stealth, moving right up to Abel Corbin, a lobbyist who was married to Grant's sister and had influence in the White House. They bought as much gold as they could get their hands on, hoping to corner the market. Their great day came on September 24—now known as Black Friday—when the market price of gold shot up at their bidding and it required government intervention to stop the panic. Hundreds of men on Wall Street claimed they had been ruined, but Gould and Fisk sold their gold before the market fell. The investigation made it clear that the blame went so high (even as high as the White House, was Fisk's unjustifiable implication) that it was difficult to make anyone responsible. These two had kept themselves in the clear. Not an order for the purchase of gold was ever made in their own names; the orders were all made in the names of their two bankrupt brokers.

"SHE'S MY DAISY."

"She's as sweet as sugar candy
And she's very fond of Andy."

CARNEGIE

Son of an immigrant labor leader from Scotland; telegraph boy who supported his family when work was short in America; avid reader of Robert Burns and Shakespeare; founder of over 2,800 libraries; ruthless businessman who became, some said, the world's richest—this unusual combination of background, ability, and character was Andrew Carnegie.

His name is now synonymous with philanthropy, but in his day it was not so kindly considered. Then it was linked with steel and money, as the cartoon indicates. An incident in which he played an important part is, oddly, one that he did not directly participate in—the steel strike in 1892 at his Homestead, Pennsylvania, plant. The strike was provoked by Henry Frick, president of Carnegie's steel company, but it had the full approval of the master. Frick wanted less union interference and lower wages for the workers. When it was time for their new contract, he arranged for steel orders to go to another plant, hired nonunion men, and brought 300 Pinkerton guards to Homestead to keep the regular workers out until they agreed to his terms. On July 6, the union men and the guards met in a bloody battle in which 13 died. The mobs ruled for five days before the state militia came, but the strike was not over until November 21. A telegram was sent to Carnegie, who had remained in Europe, not wishing to return. His short, joyous answer to Frick was "Congratulations all around—life worth living again—how pretty Italia."

MORGAN

J. PIERPONT MORGAN, UNLI
This Stirring American, Having Ga

John Pierpont Morgan was involved in the business affairs of many of the Robber Barons, and he usually handled their chaotic financial activities with dignified authority. In part, this authority had to do with his appearance, which was awesome, but it also was the result of his background. He was born into a banking family, and he turned what his father left him into a great fortune. This gave him a natural, easy assurance in comparison to men like Gould and Fisk, whose recent acquisition of money made them aggressive or showy. But Morgan was no less of a financial operator. His methods and power were feared and respected by Wall Street, making him one of the most influential and dominant figures in America.

EXANDER THE GREAT, HAS MORE WORLDS TO CONQUER.

rol of Our Railroads and Steel Business, is Reaching for the Shipping of the Universe.

His greatest success was in forming the United States Steel Corporation. By 1900, Carnegie wanted to devote more time to philanthropic and social interests, but when Morgan first suggested that he sell his steel holdings, Carnegie hesitated. He was reluctant to lose his share of the great American steel industry, but he finally agreed to sell. Carnegie's companies cost Morgan $492,000,000, and he made them, with several other companies, the basis of a huge steel trust that was capitalized at $1,404,000,000, thus beginning the era of the supertrust in American business.

When he died in 1913, Morgan left one of the world's richest banking houses— and to the Metropolitan Museum, one of the country's finest private art collections.

869

ROCKEFELLER

UNCLE JOHN.

The face of John D. Rockefeller reveals much of his character. He was determined and methodical, devoting his attention to little besides business. When he did something, it was done precisely.

His purpose was always to buy at the lowest price and sell at the greatest profit. He was able to price his oil lower than that of his competitors by demanding and getting rebates from the railroads that carried it. He then reasoned that if he had control of the refining of oil, he could dominate the market and regulate the price of oil, keeping his profits high. His first try at monopolizing the market was thwarted by independent oil producers, but this did not stop him. He undersold his competitors until, by 1878, he controlled perhaps 80% or 90% of the nation's pipelines and refineries. By 1882, he was directing all the companies affiliated with Standard Oil through a group of nine trustees who set the price and the production quotas.

As the cartoons show, the public did not look kindly on the methods of this stern man. At the left he has become Uncle Sam, with his own eagle—Senator Nelson W. Aldrich, a strong supporter. Below, the sign expresses a 1903 attitude toward the Rockefeller philanthropies.

The son of an Episcopal minister, Edward H. Harriman became a sharp speculator in railroads. At 21 he had made $3,000 and bought a seat on the Stock Exchange; by 35 he owned his first railroad; and at 49 he took over the Union Pacific, which had never recovered from Jay Gould's manipulations. He put $25,000,000 into it, and two and a half years later the road declared a dividend. Harriman then used his credit to buy other lines, and eventually he became owner of 46% of the Southern Pacific.

An attempt to take over the Chicago, Burlington & Quincy Railroad brought him into conflict with James J. Hill, the railroad master of the Northwest. Hill wanted the Burlington, as it would give him a line into Chicago and expand his railroad empire, which then consisted of the Great Northern and the Northern Pacific. Harriman did not want Hill competing with his Union Pacific. Hill went into battle with the backing of J. P. Morgan. Behind Harriman was Rockefeller. In the first round, in 1901, Hill won the Burlington by buying stock control and selling it to his Northern Pacific. But Harriman was not to be stopped. He began secretly buying Northern Pacific shares, planning in this way to control the Burlington that it owned. When Hill and Morgan discovered what was happening, they tried to counter by buying all the Northern Pacific shares on the market. This skyrocketed the price and threw the market into a panic. Finally, Morgan offered peace by creating a holding company for Hill's railroads, shares of which were owned by both sides. Harriman's cleverness and perseverance had won him a voice in the Burlington, but Hill, who was made the chairman of the new company, still directed policy.

Harriman died in 1909 at the height of his career. The cartoon gives an indication of the scope of his power in this country. He did not dominate Hill, Morgan, and Gould, as the cartoon implies, but this small, shrewd businessman could make all of them jump when he wanted.

HARRIMAN AND HILL

EDWARD H. HARRIMAN   JAMES J. HILL

MR. HARRIMAN'S PLANS FOR REORGANIZING THE RAILWAYS OF THE COUNTRY

TRY YOUR STRENGTH, GENTS!

THE HARDER YOU HIT IT, THE HIGHER IT GOES.

CHAPTER 30

THE POLITICS
OF ECONOMIC GROWTH

The growth of the Populist Party was proof that the unprecedented burgeoning of industry in post-Civil War America had left deep pockets of resentment among the populace. More aggravating still, to the vast bulk of 19th-century Americans, were the dishonesty and corruption of so many men who held or sought public office. In 1873, what one newspaperman called "the creeping, crawling things beneath the surface" of the Grant administration began to come to light. Even the solidly entrenched Republican Party could not ignore the influence-peddling, the bribetaking, and the use of high office for private gain that brought the administration of the well-meaning soldier-President into disrepute.

In a sense, the turning point of the reform movement came on July 2, 1881, at the Washington railroad station, when a disappointed office seeker named Charles J. Guiteau drew a revolver and shot the President of the United States, James A. Garfield.

A Puck *cartoonist attacks the powerful trusts as hitting the consumer with high tariffs to make their profits greater.*

One of the bullets hit the President's arm, but the other lodged in his spine, and after lingering for 79 days, he died. Following a highly publicized trial, at which the public fought for seats, the assassin was pronounced guilty and was hanged.

Although the cry for civil-service reform now became much louder, it was not altogether new. Indeed, complaints about the spoils system dated back to the administration of George Washington. Inevitably, as political parties expanded dramatically, beginning with the Jackson era, preferment came to be used increasingly to discipline party members or to attract new ones. Then, during Andrew Johnson's bitter struggle with Congress after the Civil War, the use of patronage as a political weapon became alarmingly common.

When Grant came to the Presidency, reformers renewed their efforts. In his second annual message, the President tried to persuade Congress to enact legislation governing the manner in which appointments were made. Given an appropriation of $25,000 to study the matter, Grant at once appointed an advisory committee headed by George William Curtis, the scholarly editor of *Harper's Weekly*.

The report that the Curtis committee submitted after 10 months of study must have jarred Grant. It charged, among other things, that "The business of the nation, the legislation of Congress, the duties of the departments are all subordinated to the distribution of what is well called the spoils. No one escapes. President, Secretaries, Senators, Representatives are pertinaciously dogged and besought on the one hand to appoint and on the other to retain subordinates. The great officers of the government are constrained to become mere office brokers." Although Curtis was applauded for his frankness, there was no sudden turn toward reform.

But an articulate group of reformers fought on. In 1872, some of them,

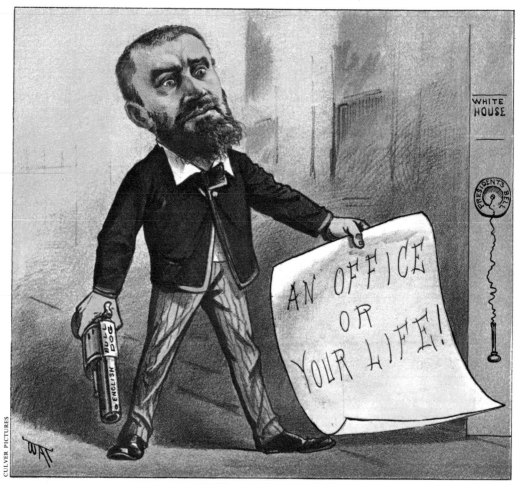

A MODEL OFFICE-SEEKER.

The face of disappointed office seeker Charles J. Guiteau, Garfield's assassin, was used in this cartoon to comment on a spoils system that was a public disgrace.

led by Missouri Senator Carl Schurz and a handful of influential Congressmen and newspaper editors, bolted the G.O.P. to form the Liberal Republican Party, with reform of the civil service its principal platform plank. The party's charge that "The civil service of the government has become a mere instrument of partisan tyranny and personal ambition, and an object of selfish greed" failed to arouse the voters enough to elect the Liberal Republicans' Presidential candidate, Horace Greeley.

Grant's two terms, during which the odor of scandal had become overpowering, had thoroughly disillusioned the electorate, and all major parties advocated reform in 1876. Presumably, no matter which won, the voter was promised some improvement.

The victor, Republican Rutherford B. Hayes, appeared to be one of those who took his party's platform seriously. Somewhat to the disappointment of old-guard Republicans, he expressed the belief that "party leaders should have no more influence in the matter of appointments than any other equally respectable citizens." He frowned upon the practice of levying political assessments upon political appointees. Even more disconcerting to those who favored business as usual was the manner in which Hayes struck out at the spoils system, particularly in New York. Senator Roscoe Conkling became highly incensed at this invasion of his territory. With heavy

Shot on July 2, 1881, four months after becoming President, Republican James A. Garfield had no time to prove his abilities.

irony he said, "When Dr. Johnson defined patriotism as the last refuge of a scoundrel, he ignored the enormous possibilities of the word 'reform.'"

As far as political integrity was concerned, Hayes' administration was a notable improvement over Grant's, but no lasting reforms were initiated. It took the assassination of Hayes' successor, Garfield, to bring matters

Claiming a tradition from three great Presidents, the Democratic Party in 1884 nominated Cleveland and Hendricks and won for the first time in 24 years.

to a head. The Republicans, frightened into action, voted for a Democratic bill presented by Senator George H. Pendleton of Ohio. The Pendleton Act, which became law early in 1883, during the administration of Chester A. Arthur, provided for a Civil Service Commission and for a classified service among a limited number of government employees. Competitive examinations henceforth were to be the basis for certain appointments.

The new law had an early test. In 1885, two years after it was passed, the Democrats swept into office. Like every winning party, they had political debts to pay. Moreover, there had not been a Democratic President since Buchanan left office in 1861; the faithful had been awaiting this victory for 24 years. In anticipation, its fruits seemed sweet.

But the new President, Grover Cleveland, was a well-known reformer whose beliefs threatened to stand in the way of the usual handouts. As it happened, Democratic Party workers need not have been concerned: Within a short time, 90% of those whose jobs depended on Presidential appointment were removed to make way for the victors; almost all of the fourth-class postmasters, for example, were let out. There were loud cries from the reformers about broken promises and the failure of the civil service law, but the critics overlooked one important fact. Less than 7% of officials already under civil service had lost their jobs, and before Cleveland left office, he had brought a new group of federal employees—those in the railroad mail service—under the protection of the Pendleton Act. In succeeding administrations the practice of generously distributing patronage continued, but as time passed, the growth of the civil service was steady and the desirability of further reforming it was unquestioned.

A tax called the tariff

Demands for tariff reform made up another strident chorus in the chant of mounting dissatisfaction over the economic situation. Earlier in the century, the tariff had been the subject of much complaint from the agricultural South; now the West took up the cause as a part of its crusade against Northeastern capital. Manufacturing interests, more powerful than at any previous time in American history, fought back fiercely. High protective tariffs not only assured them a steady profit but compensated for any wastefulness or inefficiency on their part. The leaders of organized labor, fearing the effect of cheap foreign imports on the jobs of their members, joined the fight. Users of manufactured goods, however, and particularly farmers, charged that the tariff simply amounted to another tax upon the products they wanted to buy.

For the post-Civil War generation, the tariff question dated back to the Morrill Tariff of 1861, whose schedules were steadily increased during the war. Any effort to reduce them met stiff opposition from war-born industries, whose owners argued that they could not survive without government protection.

The first postwar tariff reduction that amounted to anything came in 1872, but the financial panic of the following year cut revenues so drastically that by 1875 the schedules were again raised. By the early 1880s, however, exports and imports rose sharply, partly because of the completion of the transcontinental railroads. The federal treasury had a surplus of approximately $100,000,000, and as the tariff was to a large degree responsible, demands for tariff reduction seemed only right. The efforts of Congress in that direction were disappointing: Rates were lowered only about 4% over all, and those industries whose spokesmen complained vigorously enough managed to escape any hurtful changes.

In 1887, under the first Democratic President since before the Civil War, the tariff question was thrown squarely into the political ring. When Grover Cleveland, in his annual message to Congress that year, recommended a tariff reduction, the Democrats openly supported him. The election of 1888, it appeared, would turn upon the tariff issue.

The Republicans won with Benjamin Harrison, and they interpreted the victory as a mandate to continue the high tariff. The result was even more protection in the McKinley Tariff of 1890. Two years later, the voters strongly suggested that they did not approve the upward revision: They returned Cleveland to the White House. It now appeared that the Democrats had a mandate to lower the tariff. Their response was disheartening to those who had hope for reduction. In the Wilson Tariff of 1894, the rates on some imports were lowered, but those on others were raised, nullifying the effect of any downward trend. With the return of the Republicans to power in 1897, there followed the highly protective Dingley Tariff, which raised duties

to an average level of 57%. Thus, by the end of the century, low-tariff advocates and those who charged the protectionists with supporting monopoly could claim no progress. Industry had gained another victory. For the moment, at least, reformers could do little but lament bitterly and husband their strength for the future.

Silver vs. gold

A reform issue that rivaled the tariff question during the late 19th century revolved around a subject that has always caused arguments—money. From the close of the Civil War to the election of 1896, the "Battle of the Standards" drew the attention of increasing numbers of Americans. Simply explained, it was a contest between those who wanted an inflated currency and those who preferred a "tight money" policy.

During the early post-Civil War years, the nation's rapid economic development made serious demands upon its financial resources. American railroad mileage doubled in less than a decade; as a result, vast new areas were opened to settlement. Enormous amounts of money were required to finance the myriad new communities, and when currency appeared to be in short supply, the government was charged with failure to provide enough of it—or with adopting outright deflationary policies.

Westerners especially were incensed at the government's reluctance to encourage what Eastern bankers called

DOCTOR CLEVELAND'S PATIENTS.

Uncle Sam (*to* Civil Service Reform).—Don't cry, my child, he 'll look after you presently. Your brother needs attention more than you do.

In this cartoon, Cleveland is pictured as a sensible man who will treat the ills of the war tariffs before looking at the need for civil-service reform.

inflation. During and after the Civil War, some $400,000,000 in legal-tender notes, called "greenbacks" or "Lincoln skins," had circulated without metallic backing. In 1868, when the amount of these bills outstanding was reduced to $356,000, there were complaints from those who wanted the currency expanded rather than contracted. In 1874, Congress authorized an increase to $400,000,-000, but, to the dismay of the expansionists, President Grant vetoed the bill. In the Northeast he was, writes Matthew Josephson, "for a second time acknowledged . . . as the savior of his country." The farmers disagreed; in the Congressional elections

881

After the Civil War, the federal treasury accumulated a surplus, mostly the result of the tariffs voted in during the war. The businessman wanted tariff protection continued as it gave him greater profits, but

THE OPENING OF T

TARIFF MONSTER. — Here I am a

NGRESSIONAL SESSION.

are you going to do with me?

the users of imported goods objected because they had to pay higher prices. As this cartoon implies, the surplus and the tariff were a bugbear that appeared before every new session of Congress.

of 1878, the Greenback Party's candidates polled 1,060,000 votes.

The Greenbackers had strong allies in the free-silver advocates. In 1792, the nation's first Secretary of the Treasury, Alexander Hamilton, had suggested the free and unlimited coinage of both gold and silver at the value ratio of 15 to 1. In 1834, during Jackson's second term, the ratio was adjusted to 16 to 1. The system worked well for the rest of the century; whenever any commodity is scarce, its price will be high, and silver, not being produced in any great quantity, could be sold on the open market at such a good price that there was no great demand to have it coined.

By 1873, Congress, noting that only around 8,000,000 silver dollars had been minted since George Washington's administration, dropped that item from its coinage list. No one objected. During the late 1870s, however, the production of silver suddenly rose sharply, which meant that its value plummeted; the unprotested action of Congress in 1873 suddenly became "the crime of '73." The mountain states, whose economy leaned heavily upon silver mining, cried out loudly. Farmers, perennially in debt, saw in the free and unlimited coinage of silver the inflation and expansion of circulating media they had wanted for so long. They joined the protest. It was this alliance that made the money question political dynamite.

To meet the complaints, Richard P. Bland, a Missouri Representative, and Senator William B. Allison of Iowa sponsored a bill directing the Secretary of the Treasury to buy at least $2,000,000 worth of silver (but not more than $4,000,000 worth) per month to be coined into silver dollars. President Hayes vetoed the bill, but in the spring of 1878, it was passed over his veto. The legislation, aimed at satisfying Westerners and all others who supported currency expansion, failed to halt the falling price of silver or to produce any marked inflation of the economy.

Meanwhile, instead of issuing more greenbacks, the Republicans promised to resume the payment of specie, or hard money, for any outstanding paper notes. "Resumption," which began on January 1, 1879, meant that paper and metallic money would have the same value to the users. In the face of cries from the proponents of inflation that resumption would mean falling prices and shrinking buying power, gold and greenbacks were put on a par with each other, and after nearly two decades, the nation returned to a currency based upon metallic value. Owners of bonds and those living on fixed incomes welcomed the reappearance of "sound money." But the farmers thought they had been betrayed.

A marked economic improvement temporarily quieted Westerners. The year 1879 produced a bumper farm crop, and it was sold for record prices —a situation that had a remarkable effect upon the voters. Republican candidates swept into office in states formerly commanded by Greenbackers. So complete was the vindication of Hayes' administration that in 1880 neither party put forward any demands for free silver or inflated money.

The respite was fairly short. Hard times returned in the mid-1880s, driving agricultural prices to new lows. At the same time, the soaring production of silver depressed its price catastrophically.

In 1889 and 1890, six new states —North and South Dakota, Montana, Washington, Idaho, and Wyoming—entered the Union. All relied heavily upon either agriculture or mining, and the appearance of their representatives in Congress renewed the pressure for easy money. Eastern Republicans had not changed their minds on the subject, but they had a pet project of their own—a new tariff bill that was before Congress. The situation was ripe for a horse trade. Westerners were persuaded to vote for the McKinley Tariff of 1890; in return, Easterners reluctantly supported the Sherman Silver Purchase Act.

The Sherman Act provided that the government should buy 4,500,000 ounces of silver each month, paying the market price in treasury notes. It was no more successful than the Bland-Allison Act. Democrats opposed it on the ground that it was only a palliative, not a cure. The goldbugs sneered at it as evidence that the case for silver was hopeless. Diehard silverites condemned it as a weak

The cartoonist's stereotype of the native Irishman shows him in Dublin reading steamship notices promoting immigration.

compromise and a far cry from free and unlimited coinage. The law was in force only three years, during which approximately $156,000,000 worth of silver was bought. It was enough to stimulate some inflation, but not enough to raise farm prices appreciably. Cleveland's sponsorship of the successful effort to repeal the act brought praise from the creditor East and howls of outrage from the debtor West. His action also split the Democratic Party and threw the mon-

St. Patrick's Day was publicly celebrated as early as 1737 in Boston and 1762 in New York. Above, the 1874 New York parade marches through Union Square.

ey question squarely into the political ring, where it was snatched up by William Jennings Bryan and used as a principal weapon in his memorable, if unsuccessful, campaign of 1896.

"Give me your tired, your poor"

While industry was shooting up from infant to giant, while the West was being won, and while the country was convulsed by the inevitable growing pains, a revolution was under way. Beginning a few years before the Civil War, when the potato crop suddenly failed in Ireland, wave after wave of immigrants from Europe began landing at ports on the Eastern seaboard, drawn by the opportunity to begin life anew in a land of promise. Between 1865 and the century's end, almost 14,000,000 foreigners would arrive.

At first, native-born Americans, a naturally hospitable people whose own ancestors, after all, had been immigrants, welcomed the newcomers. Although it was written much later, Emma Lazarus' poem inscribed on the base of the Statue of Liberty proudly expressed their feelings:

> *Give me your tired, your poor,*
> *Your huddled masses yearning to*
> *breathe free . . .*

And the newcomers were useful. They built the country's roads and canals, pushed the railroads westward, and fought—on both sides—in the Civil War. They did the dirty, backbreaking jobs in mine and mill without which the industrial boom would not have been possible.

Their coming had not, it is true, been entirely free of opposition. Even before the Civil War, the Irish in Boston and Philadelphia had seen their convents and churches burned, and the Know-Nothing Party, based on anti-Catholicism and anti-foreignism, had nearly captured the Presidency. But by the 1870s and 1880s, such mindless prejudice against the Irish and the other northern Europeans—chiefly Germans and Scandinavians—who made up the early waves of immigrants had largely subsided.

The newer immigrants who followed them in a stream that seemed to have no end were from the poorer, more crowded lands of southern and eastern Europe. They were less susceptible of assimilation, it appeared; they tended to cling longer to their "foreign" ways. They crowded into the slums of Eastern cities, where, without resources, they were forced into sweatshops, with all the evils attendant upon them. Furthermore, their coming coincided with hard times, dramatized by the panics of 1873 and 1893. The day of free land in the West, which had absorbed so many of the earlier immigrants, was nearly over. Jobs were scarce in depression years, and American labor was jealous to protect those there were.

Full cooperation for a campaign to stop the entry of immigrants came from the American Protective Association, founded in the Midwest in 1887. Although it was essentially anti-Catholic in purpose, it received much support from American workers who resented the competition from southern Europeans poorer than they and therefore willing to work for less. Soon after the turn of the century, the revived Ku Klux Klan, featuring 100% Americanism, would provide additional strength to the movement.

Until the late 19th century, there had been no federal legislation aimed at control of immigration. Such regulation as there was came from the states. Then, in 1876, the United States Supreme Court handed down a decision that control must be national in character. Congress was moved to act, albeit slowly. While it pondered —some six years—nearly 2,000,000 more immigrants were admitted. Californians were particularly insistent that action be taken to stop the immigration of Chinese—which they themselves had begun by importing coolie laborers to build the Central Pacific.

The first federal immigration law was passed in 1882. Simple and brief,

This Italian family was photographed at Ellis Island in 1905 as it awaited examination by the immigration authorities.

it provided that each immigrant pay a head tax of 50¢, that the newcomers be protected against fraud and loss of their possessions upon arrival, and that all paupers, convicts, and mental defectives be excluded. The Secretary of the Treasury was empowered to make arrangements with various states for the detention of undesirables. The law was neither comprehensive nor carefully drawn, but it did establish the principle of "selection by rejection" that was to be used repeatedly until the vastly more restrictive "quota law" of 1924 virtually slammed the door shut.

Meanwhile, demands for a further tightening of regulations continued. The government responded, in 1891, with the passage of a new Federal Immigration Act, designed to bar still more would-be Americans. More classes were excluded, and steamship lines were held responsible for keeping off their vessels any persons whom the law would inevitably bar from admission once they arrived. The lines insisted they could not comply, but they managed; eventually less than 1% of those they carried were rejected. Further changes in the law excluded more groups, but strict enforcement was virtually impossible.

Restricting immigration (and in the case of the Orientals, barring an entire race) bespoke a fundamental change in national attitudes. The change coincided roughly with the closing of the frontier, suggesting for the first time that Americans had

UNCLE SAM PERSPIRES AT HIS GROWING JOB.
He Finds Turning the Crank of the Assimilation Mill is Taxing His Strength to the Utmost.

Uncle Sam is seen by the cartoonist as sweating over his backbreaking task of turning the newly arrived immigrants on Ellis Island into American citizens.

some doubt as to the illimitability of their land. The desire to shut off the "new immigration," whose source was southern European and hence Latin, was based on old feelings about the desirability of Teutonic blood, and it brought to life the cult of American nativism, dormant since Know-Nothing days.

The immigration laws ignored at least two basic realities—first, the eagerness of most of the newcomers to become good Americans and, second, the rich cultural heritage that many of them brought to the New World. No small part of America's leading musicians, scientists, inventors, scholars, and businessmen were once humble immigrants, and the country would have been much poorer without their contributions.

The fear, during World War I, that these "hyphenated Americans" (principally the German-Americans) would be disloyal to their country of adoption proved unfounded.

All these movements toward reform—of the civil service, the tariff, the monetary system, and the immigration laws—were indications that America's rapid economic growth after the Civil War had been unplanned and uneven and that the government was needed to give a guiding hand. The architects of the new industrialism, who held that their good works were not fully appreciated, believed the government was overplaying its constitutional role. The debate would continue into the 20th century —and indeed in several important ways would characterize it.

MAIN TEXT CONTINUES IN VOLUME 11

William Jennings Bryan

A SPECIAL CONTRIBUTION BY
JOHN A. GARRATY

During his 50 years of public life, Bryan ran for President three times, but at the end he was a relic of the past, an object of ridicule and pity.

"The President of the United States may be an ass," wrote H. L. Mencken during the reign of Calvin Coolidge, "but he at least doesn't believe that the earth is square ... and that Jonah swallowed the whale." The vitriolic Mencken was comparing President Coolidge to William Jennings Bryan, one of the dominant figures in the Progressive movement. According to Mencken, Bryan was an utter fraud: "If the fellow was sincere, then so was P. T. Barnum."

It was easy for sophisticates to conclude that Bryan was a fake. His undignified association with real estate promotions, his bigoted religious views, his narrow-minded attitude toward alcoholic beverages, and his unabashed political partisanship did not seem to jibe with his pretensions as a reformer. And his oratorical style, magnificent but more emotional than logical, was disappointing to thinking people. David Houston stated that "One could drive a prairie schooner through any part of his argument and never scrape against a fact."

But these flaws should never be allowed to overshadow Bryan's long years of devoted

In 1900, to Bryan's usual campaign issues— the great trusts and bimetallism—was added the imperialism born of the war with Spain.

service to the cause of reform. He was perfectly attuned to the needs and aspirations of rural America. In the early 1890s he was in the forefront of the fight against high tariffs on manufactured goods. Later in the decade he battled for currency reform. At the turn of the century he was leading the assault against imperialism. During Theodore Roosevelt's primacy he advocated a federal income tax, the eight-hour day, the control of monopoly and the strict regulation of public utilities, women's suffrage, and a large number of other startling innovations. Under Wilson he marshaled support in Congress for the Federal Reserve Act and other New Freedom measures. Whatever his limitations, few public men of his era acted as consistently "progressive" as Bryan.

For years he led the Democratic Party without holding office. Three times he was a Presidential candidate; although never elected, he commanded the loyalty of millions. He was more a man of heart than of brain, but his heart was great.

Bryan, aptly known as the Great Commoner, was a man of the people in origin and by instinct. He was born in Salem, Illinois, in 1860, a child of the great Middle West, and he absorbed its spirit and its sense of protest. After being graduated from Illinois College in 1881, he studied law in Chicago. In 1887, he moved west to Lincoln, Nebraska, where he was active in the local Democratic organization, and in 1890, at the age of 30, he won his party's nomination for Congressman.

Nebraska was traditionally a Republican state. But by 1890 tradition was rapidly

losing its hold on voters all over the Middle West. Within a single generation the United States was transformed from a land of farmers into a modern industrial society, and in the process the Middle West was caught in a relentless economic vise. Farmers, who had gone into debt during the Civil War to buy more land and machinery, watched helplessly as the prices of such staple crops as wheat plummeted from $2.50 to 50¢ a bushel. At the same time, the social status of the farmer was declining. Where once he had been a symbol of American self-reliance and civic virtue, now he was often portrayed as a hayseed—a comic mixture of shrewd self-interest and monumental provincialism. Naturally, the farmers resented their loss of both income and prestige, but there was little they could do about either.

Furthermore, the citizens of Nebraska and other agricultural states were convinced that a tiny group of powerful tycoons in great Eastern centers like Boston, New York, and Philadelphia were out to enslave the rest of the country. Useless middlemen grew fat off the mere "handling" of wheat and cotton. Monopolistic railroads overcharged for carrying crops to market; unscrupulous operators of grain elevators charged exorbitant fees. Cynical speculators drove the price of

892

At first, discontented elements concentrated on opposing the government's policy of retiring the greenbacks. To save this money, a Greenback (later Greenback-Labor) Party sprang up. Meanwhile, the Grange (originally a secret mutual-benefit association of farmers) began to agitate against the middlemen who were draining off the farmers' profits. Although the Grange abandoned political activity in the 1880s, other farm organizations quickly took its place, and around 1890 they united to form the Populist Party.

William Jennings Bryan was a Democrat, but the aspirations and the general point of view of these Midwestern farmers were his own. The farmers themselves were on the lookout for men who understood their problems. In 1888, the Republicans had carried Bryan's Congressional district by 3,000 votes; now, in 1890, the Democrat swept in with a lead of 6,713.

B ryan made an excellent record in his first term. Realizing that the money question was the crucial issue of the day, he was soon deep in a study of it, hoping to find a way to check the deflationary trend that was so injurious to his farmer constituents. He discovered that most farm-belt financial authorities thought this could best be done by providing for the free coinage of silver.

Within a month, Bryan was calling for free coinage, and he stressed the issue in his successful campaign for re-election in 1892. But the new President, Democrat Grover Cleveland, was an ardent gold-standard man, and when a severe depression struck the country early in 1893, he committed his party to the single gold standard.

Bryan, refusing to go along with this policy, threatened to "serve my country and my God under some other name" than Democrat unless the administration changed its mind.

staples up and down, without the slightest regard for the producers whose sweat made their deadly game possible.

Conspiring with bankers and mortgage holders, all these groups combined to dictate the federal government's money policy. Population and production were surging forward; more money was needed. Yet the government was deliberately cutting down on the amount of money in circulation by retiring Civil War greenbacks. On debt-ridden farmers the effect of this deflation was catastrophic.

As neither of the major parties espoused the farmers' cause wholeheartedly, the protest found its way into third-party organizations.

Although Cleveland carried the day for gold, Bryan emerged as a potential leader of the silver wing of the Democrats.

In 1894, he ran for the Senate. In those days Senators were still chosen by the state legislatures. To be elected, Bryan needed the support of Nebraska's Populists as well as that of his own party. He worked hard for fusion, but he did not get Populist support and the Republican candidate won.

Losing did not harm Bryan politically. He was still in his early 30s; to one so young, merely having run for the Senate brought considerable prestige. Also, he had conducted an intelligent and forceful campaign. Even so, it was a defeat, not calculated to lead to the remarkable decision he made— to seek nomination for the Presidency of the United States!

With Cleveland and the national organization dead set against free coinage, Bryan's chances of getting the nomination seemed infinitesimal. But if bold, his action was by no means foolish. Democratic voters were restive under Cleveland's conservative leadership. At least in Bryan's part of the nation, many Democrats were beginning to feel that they must find new leaders if they were not to be replaced by the Populists as the country's second major party. Recognizing this, Bryan proceeded to act with determination and dispatch.

He set out to make himself known beyond his own locality. Accepting the editorship of the *Omaha World-Herald,* he turned out a stream of editorials on the silver question, which he sent to influential politicians all over the country. He toured the South and West, speaking to close-packed, cheering throngs and to tiny groups of quiet listeners. His argument was simple but forceful, his oratory magnetic and compelling. Always he made sure to meet local leaders and to subject them to his genial smile, his youthful vigor, his charm, his sincerity. When the Democratic convention finally met in Chicago, Bryan believed he was known personally to more of the delegates than any other candidate.

Few delegates took his campaign seriously, but the candidate, amiable and serene, took

no offense. A majority of the delegates favored his position on silver; no one had a clear lead in the race. All Bryan needed was a chance to plead his case. The opportunity came when he was asked to close the debate on the platform's silver plank. As he came forward to address the jam-packed crowd in the Chicago auditorium, he was tense, but there was a smile on his face. He began quietly, but his voice resounded in the great hall and commanded the attention of every delegate. When he recounted the recent history of the struggle between the forces of gold and silver, the audience responded eagerly. He spoke for silver as against gold, for the West over the East, for "the hardy pioneers who have braved all the dangers of the wilderness" as against "the few financial magnates who, in a back room, corner the money of the world". He continued, "We have petitioned, and our petitions have been scorned; we have entreated, and our entreaties have been disregarded; we have begged, and they have mocked when our calamity came. We beg no longer; we entreat no more; we petition no more. We defy them!"

The crowd thundered its agreement. "Burn down your cities and leave our farms," he said, "and your cities will spring up again as if by magic; but destroy our farms and the grass will grow in the streets of every city in the country." The crowd cheered because he was reflecting its sentiments, but also because it recognized, suddenly, its leader—handsome, confident, righteously indignant, yet also calm, restrained, and ready for responsibility.

Bryan had saved a marvelous figure of speech for his climax: "We will answer their demand for a gold standard by saying to them, 'You shall not press down upon the brow of labor this crown of thorns, you shall not crucify mankind upon a cross of gold.'" Dramatically he extended his arms to the side, the very figure of the crucified Christ.

Amid the hysterical demonstration that followed, it was clear that Bryan had accom-

In 1896, in a speech at Petersburg, Virginia, Bryan claimed no man should leave his party when it is in trouble. The cartoonist points out that this is just what Bryan did in 1892.

894

HE DID NOT THINK SO IN '92.

plished his miracle. The next day, July 9, he was nominated for the Presidency on the fifth ballot.

The issue was clear-cut, for the Republicans had already declared for the gold standard and nominated thoroughly conservative William McKinley. As a result, the Populists were under great pressure to go along with Bryan. To insist on nominating a third candidate would simply insure the election of the "gold bug" McKinley. Not every important Populist favored fusion, but the rich scent of victory was in the air, and the Populist convention endorsed Bryan, too. Thus the silver forces united to do battle with the Republicans.

It was to be a close and crucial election. Seldom have the two great parties divided so clearly on fundamental issues. Silver against gold was but the surface manifestation of the struggle. City against countryside, industry against agriculture, East against South and West, the 19th century against the 20th—these were the real contestants in 1896.

After Bryan's nomination, McKinley's manager, Mark Hanna, raised huge sums by "assessing" the great bankers, oil refiners, insurance men, and meat packers, using the threat of impending business chaos and wild inflation to loosen the purse strings of the tycoons. While McKinley conducted a dignified campaign from his front porch in Canton, Ohio, 1,400 paid speakers beat the bushes for votes. The Republican campaign committee distributed more than 120,000,000 pieces of literature in 10 languages. Hanna, Theodore Roosevelt said, "has advertised McKinley as if he were a patent medicine!"

Bryan had little money and no organizational genius like Hanna to direct his drive. But between summer and November he traveled a precedent-shattering 18,000 miles, making more than 600 speeches and addressing directly an estimated 5,000,000 Americans. His secretary calculated that he spoke between 60,000 and 100,000 words every day during the campaign.

On the stump he was superb. He could make himself heard to a restless open-air throng numbered in the tens of thousands, and he was equally effective from the rear platform of a train speaking to a handful of country people. Thousands of well-wishers sent him good-luck charms and messages of encouragement. "If the people who have given me rabbits' feet in this campaign will vote for me, there is no possible doubt of my election," he said.

Such a campaign is an effective means of projecting an image and a point of view. It is not well suited for the making of complicated arguments and finely drawn distinctions. Wisely, Bryan hammered repeatedly at the currency question. He did not avoid talking about other matters: He attacked the railroads and the "tyranny" of the Eastern bankers. He deplored the use of the militia in labor disputes and the use of the injunction as a means of breaking strikes. He spoke in favor of income taxes, higher wages, and relief for hard-pressed mortgagees. But the silver issue was symbolic, the Democratic position sound, and Bryan emphasized it.

For a time his gallant, singlehanded battle seemed to be having an effect on public opinion, and Republican leaders became thoroughly frightened. Threats and imprecations now became weapons in the campaign. A rumor was circulated that Bryan was insane, and the *New York Times* devoted columns to the possibility. "Men," one manufacturer told his workers, "vote as you please, but if Bryan is elected . . . the whistle will not blow Wednesday morning." A Chicago company that held thousands of farm mortgages politely asked all its "customers" to indicate their Presidential preferences—a not very subtle form of coercion.

By election day, the McKinley managers were confident of victory, but they still put on a final monumental drive to get out the vote. Everywhere in the crucial North Central states the Hanna machine expended enormous efforts. McKinley carried all those states, and with them the nation. In the electoral college, he won by 271 to 176, but the popular vote was close—7,035,638 to 6,467,946.

The victory, however, was McKinley's, and a dividing point in the economic and social history of the United States had been crossed.

The two famous figures of the 1925 Scopes trial are shown during a recess: Clarence Darrow (left), who defended Scopes, and Bryan (right), who spoke for the prosecution.

The rural America of the 19th century was making way for the industrial America of the 20th. Soon business conditions began to improve, agricultural prices inched upward, and new discoveries of gold relieved the pressure on the money supply.

William Jennings Bryan, unchastened by defeat and always cheerful, maintained the leadership of his party. Consistently he took the liberal position on important issues. Running for President a second time in 1900, he made resistance to imperialism an issue in the campaign along with free silver. If both of these positions were poorly calculated to win votes in 1900, they were nonetheless solidly in the liberal tradition. Bryan lost to McKinley again, this time by 861,459 votes. But he continued to fight. In 1904, battling against conservatives in his own party, he forced the adoption of a fairly liberal platform (including strong antitrust, prolabor,

and antitariff planks), and when the conservative Judge Alton B. Parker was nonetheless nominated for President, Bryan kept up his outspoken criticism.

In the campaign of 1908, Bryan, once more the Democratic nominee, was defeated by William Howard Taft. Immediately he announced he would not seek the office again.

Although he thus abandoned formal leadership of the Democrats, Bryan continued to advocate reform. Throughout the Taft administration he campaigned to bolster the liberal wing of his party. When the 1912 nominating convention met in Baltimore, he threw his support to Woodrow Wilson.

Nothing reveals Bryan's fine personal qualities better than his support of Wilson, for the former Princeton professor had opposed the Great Commoner since 1896, when he had called the *Cross of Gold* speech "ridiculous."

In 1908, Wilson had refused to appear on the same platform with him. "Mr. Bryan," he said, "is the most charming and lovable of men personally, but foolish and dangerous in his theoretical beliefs." By 1912, Wilson had become far more liberal and no longer opposed most of Bryan's policies; even so, a lesser man might not have forgiven the repeated criticisms. But Bryan was more concerned with Wilson's 1912 liberalism than with personal matters, and when Wilson paid him a handsome public tribute, they became good friends. Bryan campaigned vigorously for Wilson, making well over 400 speeches within seven weeks. When Wilson won an easy victory, Bryan reacted without a trace of envy or bitterness. "It is a great triumph," he declared. "Let every Democratic heart rejoice."

Wilson made Bryan Secretary of State. He was needed in the administration to help manage his many friends in Congress. The strategy worked well; Bryan used his influence effectively. But in managing foreign affairs he was less successful, for he was ill-prepared. Because of his frank-belief in the spoils system, he dismissed dozens of key professional diplomats, replacing them with untrained political hacks. His policy of not serving alcoholic beverages at official functions because of his personal convictions caused much criticism at home and abroad. "W. J. Bryan not only suffers for his principles and mortifies his flesh, as he has every right to do," the London *Daily Express* complained, "but he insists that others should suffer and be mortified."

Unfortunately, Bryan had but a dim understanding of Latin American problems and unwittingly fostered American imperialism, causing much bad feeling in South and Central America. When World War I started in 1914, Bryan, like his chief, adopted a policy of strict neutrality. He believed in real neutrality far more deeply than Wilson, and when, after the sinking of the *Lusitania,* the President sent threatening messages to Germany, Bryan resigned as Secretary of State. He never again held public office.

It would have been better for Bryan's reputation if he had died in 1915; instead, he lived on for another decade. He made no effort to keep up with the abrupt intellectual developments of the 20th century, yet he was accustomed to speak his mind and continued to do so. More and more he confined himself to religious questions, and though his piety was heartwarming, he was a smug and intolerant Fundamentalist, ignorant of modern science and ethics.

Advancing age made Bryan even less tolerant, and he became, in the 1920s, an outspoken foe of many aspects of human freedom. He defended Prohibition, refused to condemn the Ku Klux Klan, and participated eagerly in the notorious Scopes antievolution trial, with all its overtones of censorship and self-satisfied ignorance.

The final great drama of Bryan's life occurred when Clarence Darrow mercilessly exposed his simple prejudices on the witness stand at that trial. Bryan complacently maintained that Eve was actually made from Adam's rib and that Jonah had really been swallowed by the whale. The rural audience cheered, but educated men all over the world were appalled.

Throughout his lifetime, Bryan was subject to harsh and almost continual criticism. But he was too secure in his faith to be injured by it, and he knew that for over two decades his influence was greater than that of any of his contemporaries except Theodore Roosevelt and Woodrow Wilson. His life was useful and happy, for he rightly believed that he made a lasting contribution to his country's development.

In 1896, he was indeed the peerless leader—vital, dedicated, and, in a measure, imaginative. For years the momentum of 1896 carried him on, but eventually the speeding world left him far behind. He never realized what had happened, and a few days after Darrow had exposed his shallowness before the world, he died peacefully in his sleep, as serene and unruffled by events as ever.

John A. Garraty, a professor of history at Columbia University, is the author of several full-length biographies, including those of Henry Cabot Lodge, Sr., and Woodrow Wilson.

FOR FURTHER READING

Allen, Frederick Lewis. *The Great Pierpont Morgan*. New York: Harpers, 1949. A biography that tries to deal objectively with the great banker as a person, more than as a figure in economic history.

Athearn, Robert G. *Rebel of the Rockies*. New Haven: Yale University Press, 1962. A discussion of the Denver & Rio Grande Western Railroad as part of the history of the West.

Cochran, Thomas, and Miller, William. *Age of Enterprise*. New York: Harper Torchbook. One of the basic studies of the industrial and business development of the United States.

Destler, Chester M. *American Radicalism: 1865–1901*. New London: Connecticut College, 1946. A collection of essays that examines Western radicalism in terms of the conflict between farmers and city dwellers.

Faulkner, Harold U. *Politics, Reform and Expansion*. New York: Harpers, 1959. The politics, the economic history, the efforts to reform and improve many areas of the existing society, and the new burst of territorial expansion in the decade 1890–1900.

Fish, Carl Russell. *The Civil Service and the Patronage*. New York: Longmans, Green, 1905. A leading work of civil-service reform in the latter 19th century. See chapter 2 in particular.

Griswold, Wesley. *A Work of Giants*. New York: McGraw-Hill, 1962. The building of the first transcontinental railroad.

Hibben, Paxton. *The Peerless Leader, William Jennings Bryan*. New York: Farrar and Rinehart, 1929. Chapters 16 and 17 present the views of Bryan in the election of 1896.

Hicks, John D. *The Populist Revolt*. Minneapolis: University of Minnesota Press, 1931. A basic study of Western agrarian discontent, by one of America's leading historians.

Hofstadter, Richard. *The Age of Reform: From Bryan to F.D.R.* New York: Knopf, 1955. Chapters 1 and 2 are especially perceptive in this series of essays on American intellectual history.

Holbrook, Stewart H. *The Age of the Moguls*. Garden City: Doubleday, 1956. The great promoters, bankers, industrialists, and merchants from the Civil War through World War II are portrayed as they really were.

Josephson, Matthew. *The Politicos, 1865–1896*. New York: Harcourt, Brace, 1938. A detailed chronicle of the relations between big business and politics during the reconstruction period.

Moody, John. *The Masters of Capital*. New Haven: Yale University Press, 1921. Chapters 1 through 7 emphasize the development of big business.

Nevins, Allan. *The Emergence of Modern America, 1865–1878*. New York: Macmillan, 1935. Chapter 14 includes a review of the difficulties between capital and labor during the reconstruction period.

Olcott, Charles S. *William McKinley*. 2 volumes. New York: Houghton Mifflin, 1916. An important biography of an American President. Volume 1, chapter 16 discusses the election of 1896.

Riegel, Robert E. *The Story of the Western Railroads*. New York: Macmillan, 1926. The problems of construction in the West.

Stephenson, George M. *A History of American Immigration: 1820–1924*. Boston: Ginn, 1926. The immigrants' role in the political history of the United States.

Tarbell, Ida. *The Nationalizing of Business, 1878–1898*. New York: Macmillan, 1936.

THE AMERICAN HERITAGE NEW ILLUSTRATED HISTORY OF THE UNITED STATES

PUBLISHED BY DELL PUBLISHING CO., INC.

George T. Delacorte, Jr., *Publisher* Helen Meyer, *President*
William F. Callahan, Jr., *Executive Vice-President*

Walter B. J. Mitchell, Jr., *Project Director;* Ross Claiborne, *Editorial Consultant;* William O'Gorman, *Editorial Assistant;* John Van Zwienen, *Art Consultant;* Rosalie Barrow, *Production Manager*

CREATED AND DESIGNED BY THE EDITORS OF AMERICAN HERITAGE MAGAZINE

James Parton, *Publisher;* Joseph J. Thorndike, Jr., *Editorial Director;* Bruce Catton, *Senior Editor;* Oliver Jensen, *Editor;* Richard M. Ketchum, *Editor, Book Division;* Irwin Glusker, *Art Director*

ROBERT R. ENDICOTT, *Project Editor-in-Chief*

James Kraft, *Assistant Editor;* Nina Page, Evelyn H. Register, Lynn Marett, *Editorial Assistants;* Lina Mainiero, *Copy Editor;* Murray Belsky, *Art Director;* Eleanor A. Dye, *Designer;* John Conley, *Assistant*